Duden

Einfach klasse in

Englisch

Wissen • Üben • Testen

7. Klasse

2., neu bearbeitete und erweiterte Auflage

Dudenverlag
Mannheim • Zürich

Bibliografische Information der Deutschen Nationalbibliothek
Die Deutsche Nationalbibliothek verzeichnet diese Publikation in der Deutschen Nationalbibliografie; detaillierte bibliografische Daten sind im Internet über http://dnb.d-nb.de abrufbar.

 D C B
Bibliographisches Institut GmbH
Dudenstraße 6, 68167 Mannheim

Redaktionelle Leitung Martin Bergmann
Redaktion Anika Donner, Martin Fruhstorfer
Autorin Annette Schomber
Sprecher Alison Ripier, Michael Shiels

Herstellung Annette Scheerer
Layout Horst Bachmann
Illustration Carmen Strzelecki
Umschlaggestaltung WohlgemuthPartners, Bremen
Umschlagabbildung Plainpicture

Satz Katrin Kleinschrot, Stuttgart
Druck und Bindung Heenemann GmbH & Co. KG
Bessemerstraße 83–91, 12103 Berlin
Printed in Germany

ISBN 978-3-411-72272-3

Inhaltsverzeichnis

INHALT

INHALT

1 Substantive und Artikel

1.1 Zählbare und nicht zählbare Substantive

Zählbare Substantive

Die regelmäßigen Pluralformen der **zählbaren Substantive** *(countable nouns)* werden durch Anhängen von *-s* gebildet.	a friend – a lot of friend**s** my pencil – those pencil**s**
Aufgepasst: Endet ein Substantiv auf *-s, -ss, -sh* oder *-ch,* wird *-es* angehängt.	one bus – four bus**es** a watch – their watch**es**
Besonderheiten der Schreibweise im Plural: ■ Nach einem **Konsonanten** wird *-y* zu *-ies,* nach einem **Vokal** bleibt *-y* erhalten. ■ Bei Substantiven auf *-f*/*-fe* wird der Plural meist auf *-ves* gebildet. ■ Einige Substantive auf *-o* haben im Plural *-oes.*	famil**y** – famil**ies,** bab**y** – bab**ies** *Aber:* bo**y** – bo**ys** shel**f** – shel**ves,** kni**fe** – kni**ves** *Aber:* roof – roof**s,** chief – chief**s** potat**o** – potat**oes,** tomat**o** – tomat**oes** *Aber:* phot**o** – phot**os,** radi**o** – radi**os**

Nicht zählbare Substantive

Nicht zählbare Substantive *(uncountable nouns)* kommen nur im Singular vor. Sie stehen mit unbestimmten Mengenangaben.	I need **some** water. There is **no** butter in the fridge. My friend usually has **a little** sugar in her tea.
Will man sie zählbar machen, muss ein zählbares Substantiv hinzugefügt werden.	four cups of tea, a slice of bread, six bottles of water
Merke: **Getränke** werden oft zu zählbaren Substantiven, wenn sie zum Beispiel in einem Restaurant bestellt werden.	Two coffees, please. (*statt:* two cups of coffee) Could I have a beer, please? (*statt:* a glass of beer)
Aufgepasst: Einige Substantive, die nicht zählbar sind, haben auch eine zählbare Form. Die zählbare Form hat dann jedoch eine **andere Bedeutung.**	Your **hair** (Frisur) looks lovely today. There are some **hairs** (einzelne Haare) on your shirt. Do you like **sport** (Sport)? My favourite **sports** (Sportart) is tennis.

Gruppenbezeichnungen

Gruppenbezeichnungen *(collective nouns)* können sowohl im Singular als auch im Plural gebraucht werden:	
family, club, group, class, band, team, crew, army	My family **has / have** already arrived.
Im Singular wird die Gruppe als **Ganzes** betont, steht der Plural, ist der **Einzelne** in der Gruppe gemeint.	The band **is / are** putting its / their instruments away. **Is / Are** Mr Clark's class difficult to teach?
Es gibt Gruppenbezeichnungen, die immer mit dem **Plural** gebraucht werden:	
people – die Leute *the police – die Polizei* *cattle – Vieh, Rinder*	There were only a few people in the shop. The police have just caught the thief. The cattle are hungry.
Aufgepasst: People als zählbares Substantiv hat eine andere Bedeutung.	Are they a peace-loving people (ein friedliebendes Volk)? The peoples of Africa (die Völker Afrikas) speak different languages.
Einige Substantive haben keinen Singular. Sie kommen nur im **Plural** vor.	clothes – stairs – looks – thanks
Pronomen und Verben, die mit diesen Pluralwörtern kombiniert werden, werden ebenfalls im Plural benutzt.	Clothes (die Kleidung) are really cheap here. These stairs (diese Treppe) lead to my room. Her looks (ihr Aussehen) haven't changed.

Paarwörter

Für Dinge, die aus zwei gleichen Teilen bestehen, verwendet man ein Substantiv im Plural.	trousers – shorts – leggings – tights – jeans – scissors – pyjamas – glasses – headphones
Diese **Paarwörter** *(pair nouns)* stehen immer im Plural und können deshalb niemals mit dem unbestimmten Artikel oder mit Zahlen verwendet werden.	I have bought new jeans. Your pyjamas are great. Where did you get them?
Sie werden mit Verben in der Pluralform verbunden. Mengenangaben wie ***a / one pair of*** oder ***two / three ... pairs of*** machen Paarwörter zählbar.	My father needs a new pair of glasses. Have you packed your two pairs of trousers?

WISSEN

ÜBUNG 1 **Zählbar oder nicht zählbar? Ordne die Gegenstände dem richtigen Feld zu.**

zählbar

nicht zählbar

ÜBUNG 2 **Gruppenbezeichnungen: Bilde Sätze mit dem Verb, einmal im Singular und einmal im Plural.**

My family – to go – France – every year

My family goes / go to France every year.

class 5 MC – to want to visit – museum – in York

computer club – usually – to meet – on Fridays

Sam's favourite team – often – to win

the band – just – to start to play – in the concert hall

ÜBEN

ÜBUNG 3 **Paarwörter: Schreibe auf, was die jeweiligen Personen besitzen.**

ÜBUNG 4 **Finde passende Mengenangaben zu den nicht zählbaren Substantiven.**

~~sugar~~ – sand – money – meat – soup – bread – ketchup – water – butter

a pound of sugar,

ÜBUNG 5 **Lies die Sätze und unterstreiche die richtige Form.**

Do you really want to wear a jeans / some jeans?

Where did you get this / these fantastic headphones?

Many / Much thanks for your help.

You can always buy another shorts / another pair of shorts.

Where is / are my pyjamas? – I think I've already packed them / it.

£ 15 for a pair of scissors / a scissors! It is / They are really expensive.

ÜBUNG 6 **Vervollständige die Sätze mit den richtigen Substantiven, Verbformen und Pronomen.**

I can't find my  ____________ . Have you seen ____________ ? –
Yes, here they ____________ (to be).

The 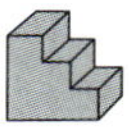 ____________ in that house ____________ (to be) dangerous. – I know, ____________ (to be) very old and almost broken.

Look at that accident over there. We should call  ____________ . –
Okay, I'll call ____________ .

The  ____________ you lent me ____________ (not to cut) very well.

Your  ____________ ____________ (to look) great.

Show me your new  ____________ . – Here ____________ (to be). Do you like ____________ ?

 ____________ ____________ (to be) kept for their milk and meat.

ÜBUNG 7 **Finde die Fehler in den folgenden Sätzen und schreibe den verbesserten Satz in dein Übungsheft. Achtung: Einige Sätze sind korrekt!**

Do you want coffee?
I haven't got a pen.
Sarah drinks a water every day.
My friends often listen to music when they work.
Look at all those hairs on your new anorak.
We need a milk and four eggs.
Would you like some breads?

ÜBUNG 8 **Übersetze die folgenden Sätze ins Englische und schreibe sie in dein Übungsheft.**

Ich brauche eine neue Strumpfhose und einen Schlafanzug.
Es sind heute viele Leute im Park.
Trägt Liz gewöhnlich eine Brille?
Meine Familie trinkt jeden Tag mehrere Flaschen Wasser.
Ich hätte gerne Schokolade und etwas Brot.

1.2 Der Artikel

Der bestimmte Artikel

Der bestimmte Artikel *(the definite article)* ***the*** wird benutzt,	
■ wenn eine **Person** oder eine **Sache** näher bestimmt ist,	The people in our street are very friendly. We live in the house over there.
■ wenn **abstrakte Begriffe** *(life, love, happiness, peace, hate, death)* durch einen Relativsatz oder eine *of-phrase* näher erläutert werden,	The life of Robin Hood was full of adventures. The love that you can find between them ...
■ wenn bei Institutionen *(church, school, university, prison)* das **Gebäude** und nicht die Funktion gemeint ist,	She parked her car in front of the school. The new supermarket is near the church.
■ bei **Eigennamen** von Flüssen, Meeren, Museen, Theater, Hotels, Kinos, Eigennamen mit *of* und Eigennamen im Plural.	the Thames, the Atlantic, the British Museum, the Odeon Cinema, the Hilton Hotel, the Tower of London, the Millers, the Highlands, the Alps
Der bestimmte Artikel wird nicht benutzt,	
■ wenn **abstrakte Begriffe** im allgemeinen Sinn gebraucht werden,	Life can be hard sometimes. Love makes the world go round.
■ wenn bei Institutionen die **Funktion** des Gebäudes gemeint ist,	Most pupils don't go to school on Saturday. The thieves went to prison for one year.
■ bei **Eigennamen** von Seen, Gebirgen, Straßen, Parks, Brücken, Plätzen und vielen Gebäuden und Ländern sowie Eigennamen mit Adjektiven,	near Loch Ness, in Bond Street, around Piccadilly Circus, in front of Buckingham Palace, in England, modern Britain, poor Tim
■ bei Monaten, Wochentagen, Feiertagen und Mahlzeiten.	in June, on Tuesday, at Christmas / Easter, after breakfast

Der unbestimmte Artikel

Der unbestimmte Artikel *(the indefinite article)* wird benutzt,	
■ wenn keine bestimmte Person oder Sache gemeint ist,	Yesterday I met a very nice lady. They have bought a new car.
■ bei Nationalitäten und Berufen,	Is he an Englishman? Her mother is a vet.
■ bei Verbindungen mit *half, quite, such* und *what*.	half an hour – such a nice boy – quite a good film – what a lovely day

ÜBUNG 9 **Vervollständige die Sätze mit dem bestimmten Artikel dort, wo er nötig ist. Aufgepasst: Oft ist kein Artikel nötig!**

I'm thirsty. Where is ______ coke I bought yesterday? – ______ Coke / coke isn't good for you. Why don't you drink ______ water?

______ Sandwiches / sandwiches you made were fantastic, Kate. I didn't know you could make ______ sandwiches so well.

______ Life / life in England wasn't easy in the 16th century, not even ______ life of a king or queen.

Sometimes ______ people don't know what is right. ______ People / people who live in our street are usually very loud. ______ People / people can be so unfriendly.

ÜBUNG 10 **Höre dir Track 1 auf der CD an und ergänze das fehlende Nomen und den Artikel, falls dieser notwendig ist.**

1

______ that I go to has a lot of pupils. I don't like big schools. Well, I don't like ______ anyway, but my parents think that ______ is important for my future.

Sarah lives in a big town. There's a prison and a university. Sarah's sister goes to ______ because she wants to become a doctor. ______ is not far from ______.

Jim likes football. On his way home from ______ he often plays it with his friends. Last year he broke his left arm playing football and he had to go to ______. The best thing about breaking his arm was that he didn't have to go to ______ or to ______. Some of Jim's friends live close to ______. He sometimes meets them after ______.

ÜBUNG 11 **Wähle eine passende Definition für jeden Begriff und vervollständige die Sätze. Vergiss den unbestimmten Artikel nicht.**

A duck is a bird.

A carrot is ______.

Tennis is ______.

Mount Everest is ______.

ÜBEN

ÜBUNG 12 **Vervollständige die folgenden Sätze, indem du die passenden Begriffe in den Wortspeichern zusammenfügst.**

quite – such – half – what – such – quite

a beautiful dress – a stupid thing to do – an easy question – a lovely meal – a useful thing – an hour later

I have never eaten ______________ .

Look at these clothes. ______________ .

Tim, you must be more careful. It was ______________ .

It was raining heavily, but ______________ it stopped suddenly.

We can do our homework quickly. It is ______________ .

A penknife is ______________ , because you can take it everywhere.

WISSEN+

Redewendungen mit dem unbestimmten Artikel
Eine Reihe von feststehenden Ausdrücken hat immer den unbestimmten Artikel bei sich:

to be in a hurry – to have a headache / a cold / a temperature – to take a shower / a bath – to take a seat – to take a holiday – to make a noise – for a long time – in a loud voice – what a pity

Did you take a shower today?
I haven't been here for a long time.
He doesn't feel well, I think he has a temperature.

ÜBUNG 13 **Wähle aus dem Wissen+-Kasten die richtige Redewendung aus, um die nachstehenden Sätze zu vervollständigen. Schreibe die Sätze in dein Übungsheft.**

Sarah must stay in bed. She ...
Jane had a busy day at work. She wants to ...
The Masons' friends came in and ...
"Jeff isn't allowed to come to my party." – "..."
Luke was really angry. He said ...: "How dare you!"

ÜBUNG 14 **Vervollständige die Sätze, indem du die rot markierten Ausdrücke übersetzt.**

What did you have zum Frühstück? →

I didn't do anything am letzten Wochenende. →

What would you like zum Mittagessen? →

Where will you spend your holidays im nächsten Sommer? →

Can she visit you im Oktober? →

Let's go to the cinema am Freitagabend. →

Would you like to go swimming am Nachmittag? →

Can we watch a DVD nach dem Abendessen? →

They often go on holiday im Juli. →

ÜBUNG 15 **Setze entweder den bestimmten Artikel *the* oder den unbestimmten Artikel *a / an* ein. Wenn kein Artikel erforderlich ist, lasse die Lücke frei.**

Who is ______ best player in your team?

I don't watch ______ TV in the evening.

Is there ______ supermarket near here? – Yes, it is at ______ end of the street.

Do you live here or are you ______ tourist?

What did you have for ______ breakfast?

Do you play ______ piano?

What time is ______ train to Edinburgh?

Kate never writes ______ letters. She prefers to phone people.

Where's Sue? – She is in ______ house.

Julia was sick ______ last week, so she couldn't go to ______ school.

Have you ever been to ______ Bond Street?

Last year the Dicksons had ______ wonderful holiday in the north of ______ England.

Klassenarbeit 1

45 Minuten

AUFGABE 1 **Ordne die folgenden Substantive der richtigen Zeile zu.**

team – ice cream – glasses – bottle – chocolate – tights – hair – milk – stairs – child – choir – box – sugar – people – cattle – house – beach – jeans – police

zählbare Substantive: _____

nicht zählbare Substantive: _____

Gruppenbezeichnungen: _____

Pluralwörter: _____

Paarwörter: _____

AUFGABE 2 **Plural oder Singular? Setze jeweils das richtige Bestimmungswort und / oder die richtige Form der Gegenwart des Verbs in den Klammern ein.**

_____ (This / These) stairs _____ (to be) broken. The shorts _____ (to be) new. Tom's trousers _____ (to be) too long. _____ (This / These) homework _____ (to be) really easy. The police usually _____ (to come) when you call _____ (it / them). Do you like _____ (this / these) clothes?

AUFGABE 3 **Kate im Supermarkt. Was hat sie alles eingekauft?**

Kate has just bought two bottles of _____ _____ _____ _____.

AUFGABE 4 **Unterstreiche die Fehler in den folgenden Sätzen und verbessere sie, indem du den ganzen Satz neu in dein Übungsheft schreibst.**

ACHTUNG FEHLER

Tim has got green eyes and black hairs.

Sarah usually wears a cool sunglasses.

There is a milk on the table.

I have just bought a cheese at the supermarket.

Mrs Hill wants to buy two shorts for her summer holidays next week.

Can I have three coffee, please?

AUFGABE 5 ***The, a / an*** **oder kein Artikel – entscheide dich.**

Bill takes ______ bath every morning and has cornflakes for ______ breakfast.

Jenny can't go to ______ school today. She has got ______ headache and ______ temperature.

______ Poor / poor Mr Jenkins. He broke his leg after ______ breakfast.

Sarah is on her way to ______ school. ______ School / school is opposite the museum.

Jane likes music. In ______ afternoons she often plays ______ guitar.

We usually go on holiday in ______ July.

What ______ lovely day! The sun is shining and we can play outside.

Janet wants to become ______ teacher.

AUFGABE 6 **Übersetze die rot markierten Satzteile ins Englische und schreibe den gesamten Satz noch einmal in dein Übungsheft.**

Meine Brille ist broken. →

Das Vieh ist in the stalls. →

John has got drei Jeans. →

Die Treppe ist high. →

Is der Buckingham Palace in London? →

After school I would like to go an die Universität. →

Das Leben can be difficult sometimes. →

TESTEN

Klassenarbeit 2

45 Minuten

AUFGABE 7 **Wähle aus dem Wortspeicher das richtige Substantiv und schreibe es in der Pluralform in die richtige Lücke.**

coffee – knife – city – bus – story – country – radio – boy – thief – tomato

Some children like reading ______ about ghosts and fairies.

Kevin's friends are from many different ______ all over the world.

London, Paris and Berlin are big ______.

May we have three ______, please – without milk.

The ______ are often late these days. I might go by car again.

Those ______ haven't been caught yet.

Here are the ______ to slice the ______.

The ______ are listening to their ______.

AUFGABE 8 **Entscheide dich für *is* oder *are* in den folgenden Sätzen.**

Your hair ______ pretty long.

The police ______ very helpful here.

The bars of chocolate ______ in the cupboard.

The cattle ______ outside.

This band ______ really famous.

The box of toys ______ in Timmy's room.

AUFGABE 9 **Schreibe die folgenden Sätze um, indem du die unterstrichenen Satzteile mit einer *of-phrase* zählbar machst.**

May I have <u>some bread</u> please? May I have two ______, please?

How much <u>lemonade</u> do we need? – I think we need ten ______.

Let's have <u>some coffee</u>. I'll get us four ______.

You mustn't forget <u>the soap</u>. Two ______ will be enough.

Dorothy likes <u>milk</u>. She has three ______ for breakfast.

AUFGABE 10 **Schreibe dort den bestimmten Artikel vor den Eigennamen, wo er notwendig ist.**

United Kingdom	Buckingham Palace
Hyde Park	Pacific Ocean
River Rhine	Jupiter
Odeon Cinema	Ritz
Ground Zero	Great Lakes
Republic of China	M5

AUFGABE 11 **Vervollständige die folgenden Sätze mithilfe des Wortes in Klammern. Benutze den bestimmten Artikel immer dort, wo er notwendig ist.**

Bob broke his arm last week. He's (hospital) .

On Sundays our neighbours usually go (church) .

Can we park our car right in front (prison) ?

We have just heard (terrible news) (radio) .

When should teenagers go (bed) ?

Mum is having a shower (bathroom) .

He goes (work / bike) .

When did they arrive (airport / New York) ?

AUFGABE 12 **Bilde Sätze! Benutze dabei die Satzteile aus dem linken und rechten Kasten. Vergiss den bestimmten oder unbestimmten Artikel nicht, wenn dieser notwendig ist. Schreibe in dein Übungsheft.**

We arrived at	sea
Have you ever seen	Bond Street
He loves playing	work the teacher gave them
The cyclist was injured and taken to	Euston Station
My friend has	piano
Last year Jeff started to work as	Himalayas
Who fell into	good job
The pupils have just finished	doctor in a hospital
Who was the first man on	hospital
They met in	Moon

2.1 Die Reflexivpronomen

Formen der Reflexivpronomen

Die **Formen** der Reflexivpronomen *(reflexive pronouns)* enden im Singular auf *-self* und im Plural auf *-selves.*

Singular		
I	*myself*	Oh dear! I have cut myself.
you	*yourself*	Did you make the cake yourself?
he, she	*himself / herself*	Darren can repair his bike himself. She is washing herself.
it	*itself / oneself*	One might cut oneself. The dog can open the door itself.
Plural		
we	*ourselves*	We painted the house ourselves.
you	*yourselves*	Have you hurt yourselves?
they	*themselves*	They can cook supper themselves.

Aufgepasst: Die Reflexivpronomen werden auf der zweiten Silbe betont.

Gebrauch der Reflexivpronomen

Reflexivpronomen werden folgendermaßen gebraucht:

- Das Reflexivpronomen **bezieht sich** auf das Subjekt eines Satzes **zurück:** Das Objekt bezeichnet dieselbe Person wie das Subjekt.
  He cut himself (sich) with a knife.
  My father is teaching himself (sich) English.
  Their children can look after themselves (um sich).
- Das Reflexivpronomen wird auch verwendet, wenn man ein Nomen oder Pronomen eines Satzes **hervorheben** will.
  The castle itself (das Schloss selbst, an sich) is very interesting.
  He himself (er selbst) was driving.
  They spoke to her themselves (sie redeten selbst mit ihr).

Reflexivpronomen stehen in einigen **festen Wendungen.**

Enjoy yourself! – Viel Spaß! Amüsier dich!
Help yourselves! – Bedienen Sie sich!
I did it by myself. – Ich habe es allein getan.

ÜBUNG 1 **Setze die richtigen Reflexivpronomen ein.**

Mrs Gray hasn't got a teacher. She is teaching __________ French.

He was looking at __________ in the mirror.

I'm not angry with you. I'm angry with __________ .

My parents had a great time in New York. They enjoyed __________ .

We are old enough to look after __________ .

The sandwiches are on the table. Just help __________ , boys.

I didn't buy those pies. I made them __________ .

Matthew never thinks about other people. He only thinks about __________ .

ÜBUNG 2 **Was können die Personen nicht selbst machen? Schreibe zu jedem Bild einen Satz und benutze das richtige Reflexivpronomen.**

to carry bags

to wash his hair

to repair a bike

to get down

The old lady can't __________ .

__________ .

__________ .

__________ .

ÜBUNG 3 **Höre dir Track 2 auf der CD zweimal an und setze die fehlenden Reflexivpronomen ein. Unterstreiche die, die der Verstärkung dienen.**

2

They did the exercises ______ .

My brother doesn't want to clean my father's car ______ .

Listen! Rita is talking to ______ .

I don't know the answer ______ . Can you help me, please?

Be careful! You may hurt ______ really badly.

Timmy has made all those sandwiches ______ . Isn't he a sweet boy?

WISSEN

Reflexives oder nicht reflexives Verb?
Viele Verben, die im Deutschen reflexiv sind, werden im Englischen nicht reflexiv gebraucht:

to hurry – sich beeilen, to move – sich bewegen, to sit down – sich setzen, to hide – sich verstecken, to open – sich öffnen, to change – sich ändern, to happen – sich ereignen, to apologize – sich entschuldigen, to remember – sich erinnern, to wonder – sich fragen, to concentrate – sich konzentrieren, to worry – sich Sorgen machen, to imagine – sich etwas vorstellen, to be afraid of – sich fürchten

Sit down and don't move!
She couldn't concentrate.
What happened? – I can't remember.
Nothing has changed.
Don't worry.
Hurry up!
They met in the park.
I can't remember.

ÜBUNG 4 **Übersetze die rot hervorgehobenen Wörter.**

He ______ (kann sich nicht leisten) a new bike.

Sally ______ (konnte sich nicht erinnern) where she had put the keys.

Just ______ (stell dir vor) the world would stop turning.

She ______ (hat sich verändert) a lot over the past years.

I ______ (entschuldige mich) for being late.

ÜBEN

ÜBUNG 5 **Lies die Sätze durch, suche ein passendes Verb aus dem Wortspeicher aus und entscheide, in welchen Sätzen die Verben ein Reflexivpronomen benötigen.**

to help – to enjoy – to hide – to meet – to open – to relax –
to change – to remember – to move – to be afraid

The window ______ , and a girl climbs in.

You must be tired. Just ______ and ______ .

Are we ______ at 7 o'clock for dinner?

Don't ______ . Everything will turn out right.

Look at that tree over there. Its branches are ______ in the wind.

She wants to ______ before she goes for a walk.

We ______ to some drinks and sandwiches.

I can't ______ . I have never seen that film before.

Where ______ you ______ ? I can't see you!

ÜBUNG 6 **Übersetze die folgenden Sätze ins Englische und benutze das richtige Reflexivpronomen. Achte darauf, dass im Englischen nicht immer das Reflexivpronomen stehen muss!**

Ich habe dieses Kleid selbst gekauft.

______

Sei vorsichtig mit der neuen Schere. Du kannst dich schneiden.

______

Wir müssen uns keine Sorgen machen.

______

Anne und Luke haben sich sehr amüsiert.

______

Er beeilte sich, weil er sich im Dunkeln fürchtete.

______

2.2 Reziproke Pronomen und das Stützwort *one / ones*

Reziproke Pronomen

Each other und ***one another*** sind reziproke Pronomen *(reciprocal pronouns)*. Sie werden verwendet, wenn eine Handlung auf **Gegenseitigkeit** beruht.

Bei mehreren Personen kann man statt *each other* auch *one another* verwenden.

Bob and Liz are helping each other with their homework.
Do you send each other birthday cards?
People often write one another on christmas.

Im Englischen wird unterschieden, ob eine **wechselseitige Beziehung** vorliegt *(each other / one another)*, oder ob eine Handlung **reflexiv** ist und sich auf das Subjekt des Satzes bezieht: Dann steht das **Reflexivpronomen** (↑ Kap. 2.1).

Im Deutschen wird in beiden Fällen „sich" übersetzt.

Lucy is looking at Ben and Ben is looking at Lucy. Lucy and Ben **are looking at each other** (= sie sehen sich gegenseitig an).

Lucy is looking in the mirror. She **is looking at herself** in the mirror (= sie sieht sich selbst an).

Das Stützwort *one / ones*

Soll ein zählbares Substantiv nicht wiederholt werden, so kann es durch das Stützwort *(prop-word)* ***one / ones*** ersetzt werden.

One steht beim Singular, *ones* beim Plural.

Can I have a new pen? – No, we bought **one** last week.
I've had these shoes for ages. I really need some new **ones.**

Merke: Im Englischen können der bestimmte Artikel oder Adjektive – anders als im Deutschen – nicht alleine stehen. Sie benötigen *one / ones* als Stützwort.

Which of these pullovers do you like best? – The red **one.** (den roten)
These T-shirts are nice. – I like the blue **ones.** (die blauen)

ÜBUNG 7 **Vervollständige die Sätze mit *each other / one another*.**

They like ______________________ very much.

They have just given ______________________ presents.

Mr and Mrs Miller shout at ______________________ a lot.

ÜBUNG 8 **Vervollständige die folgenden Sätze und verwende entweder *each other / one another* oder das richtige Reflexivpronomen.**

Paul and I live near ______________ .

You can help Tom and Tom can help you. So you and Tom can help ______________ .

There's food in the kitchen. If you are hungry, you can help ______________ .

When we go to the zoo, we always enjoy ______________ .

Mary and Jane were at school together but they never see ______________ now.

A lot of people talk to ______________ when they are alone.

Jill, Mary and Sue are good friends. They know ______________ well.

Steve has got a new penfriend. Do they often write to ______________ ?

Mr Benson, I'll do that. I'd like to do it ______________ .

A lot of children hurt ______________ when they get off their bikes too quickly.

Husband and wife should always tell ______________ the truth.

ÜBUNG 9 **Vervollständige die Sätze unten mit den Satzteilen im Wortspeicher. Achte auf die richtige Verwendung der reziproken Pronomen und Reflexivpronomen!**

look after each other – look after themselves – talk to each other – talk to themselves – help each other – help yourselves

When old friends meet, they often __________.

Young and fit people can __________.

People who live alone often start to __________.

First she was ill in bed, then he was ill, so they had to __________.

Fred and Sheila phone every day to __________ with their homework.

Please __________. Everything you need is on the table.

ÜBUNG 10 **Vervollständige die Sätze, indem du das Stützwort *one / ones* benutzt.**

Can you lend me your pen? – I'm sorry, I haven't got __________.

This cup is dirty. Can I have a clean __________?

Which trousers do you like? These __________ or those __________?

This box is too small. I need a bigger __________.

Those shoes are much nicer than the blue __________.

WISSEN +

Das Stützwort ***one / ones*** kann in folgenden Fällen **entfallen:**

■ nach dem Superlativ eines Adjektivs,	The green shirt is the most expensive (one).
■ nach Ordnungszahlen,	Were you the first (one) to arrive?
■ nach einem Demonstrativpronomen,	I think this poster is nicer than that (one).
■ nach *any, another, either, neither, each,*	There are five dogs. Each (one) likes dog biscuits.
■ nach *which.*	We have all these colours. Which (one) do you like?

ÜBEN

ÜBUNG 11 **Entscheide, wann in der folgenden Übung das Stützwort *one / ones* notwendig ist. Wenn du das Stützwort weglassen kannst, lasse die Lücke leer.**

Which ______ would you like: the expensive sunglasses or the cheap ______ ?

Which of the two cities is the bigger ______ : London or New York?

If you see a nice pullover, could you get me ______ , please?

My dog is the nicest ______ in the world.

I'm going to buy this ______ , not that ______ .

How many fish did you catch? – I caught three big ______ .

Jim is wearing nice shoes, but Joe is wearing bigger ______ .

Linda was the third ______ to come in time.

My little sister got a rabbit for her birthday. It's a black ______ .

My brother has got three cats. Each ______ is cute.

Would you like the black one or the white one? – Both ______ , please.

ÜBUNG 12 **Findest du die Fehler in den folgenden Sätzen? Wenn du sie entdeckt hast, schreibe den korrigierten Satz noch einmal vollständig ab.**

ACHTUNG FEHLER

Which apples shall we buy? The red?

I have just met Sue in town. We haven't seen ourselves for ages.

Jim is carrying heavy parcels, but Terry is carrying heavier.

How many towers did this skyscraper have? – I think it had two identical one.

George writes Terry, and Terry writes George. So they write.

Klassenarbeit 1

45 Minuten

AUFGABE 1 **Fülle die Lücke entweder mit einem Reflexivpronomen oder einem reziproken Pronomen.**

Look at your hand. You have cut ______ with the knife.

Billy and Jeff don't do anything together. I don't think they like ______ .

Tom and Jenny always help ______ with the washing-up.

How was the concert? Did you enjoy ______ , Tina?

Some people like talking about ______ all the time.

He did it by ______ .

AUFGABE 2 **Setze das richtige Pronomen ein. Achtung: Manchmal darf keines stehen! Lasse die Lücke dann leer.**

Billy doesn't have a Spanish teacher. He is teaching ______ Spanish.

Jeff and I met ______ in town this morning.

Janet fell off the skateboard and broke ______ her left arm.

You must learn to concentrate ______ .

My parents have known ______ for about thirty years.

I was so tired I had to sit down ______ .

If you arrive late, you must apologise ______ .

The oven is still hot. Don't touch it! You might burn ______ .

AUFGABE 3 **In jedem der folgenden Sätze ist ein Fehler. Markiere ihn und verbessere ihn in deinem Übungsheft. Aufgepasst: Ein Satz ist richtig!**

ACHTUNG FEHLER

We are late, so we must hurry ourselves.
Be careful, don't cut you with that bread knife.
Your friends are really nice now. They have changed themselves a lot.
You can't look at each other because the mirror is broken.
My mum always worries when I'm with my friends.
Can I get me a drink?
Sally, look at those trousers. I like the blue one.

AUFGABE 4 **Entscheide dich für das richtige Pronomen und unterstreiche es.**

Friends usually give themselves / each other presents at Christmas.

Anna and I don't see us / ourselves / each other very often.

My brother always cuts his hair – / himself.

Stop talking about you / – / yourself. That's boring.

While Mary and John were talking to each other / themselves they were looking at each other / themselves.

He can't imagine – / himself what might happen next.

AUFGABE 5 **Du gehst mit deinem englischen Austauschschüler einkaufen. Vervollständige die Fragen mit *one / ones* und den angegebenen Adjektivpaaren.**

green / red - Swiss / French - old / new - brown / white - chocolate / plain

Which cheese should we buy – the ______ or the ______ ?

Which apples shall we get – ______ ?

Which biscuits do you prefer – ______ ?

Which eggs do you want – ______ ?

Which car belongs to you – ______ ?

AUFGABE 6 **Bilde aus den folgenden Wörtern Sätze und schreibe sie in dein Übungsheft. Ergänze das fehlende Reflexivpronomen, reziproke Pronomen oder Stützwort, falls notwendig. Achte auch auf die richtige Satzstellung!**

Cats / to clean / every day
Mike / to enjoy / usually / at parties
I / not to feel / very well / at the moment
Pat and Jill / to understand / without saying anything
There / to be / red apple and / a green
Sally's friends / to play with / often / a game of cards

Klassenarbeit 2

45 Minuten

AUFGABE 7 **Beantworte die folgenden Fragen, indem du in den Antworten ein Reflexivpronomen wählst. Das einleitende Personalpronomen in der Antwort hilft dir dabei.**

Who has made these sandwiches? – We have made them ______ .

Who will organise the next bring-and-buy sale? – I will organise it ______ .

Who has built those sandcastles? – They have built them ______ .

Who drives this car? – She drives it ______ .

Who arranged the meeting? – He arranged it ______ .

Who washed the dirty pullover? – You washed it ______ .

AUFGABE 8 **Schreibe die Sätze um, indem du das passende Reflexivpronomen verwendest.**

Sue has cut her hand with a knife. She has cut ______ with a knife.

They went to Italy without their parents. They went to Italy ______ .

I was sitting in that room. There was nobody else. I was sitting ______ .

Tina made biscuits and nobody helped her. She made biscuits all ______ .

The girls are looking at their reflection in the mirror. They are looking at ______ in the mirror.

The party was great fun. We enjoyed ______ .

AUFGABE 9 **Unterstreiche das richtige Pronomen in den folgenden Sätzen.**

Bob and Fiona must be in love because they look at each other / at themselves quite often.

Help yourselves / each other to the coffee and cake.

Pupils in my class often help each other / themselves when an exercise is really difficult.

I write to my pen friend and he writes to me, so we often write to each other / ourselves.

The Smiths cooked a delicious meal for each other / themselves at Christmas.

We are still fit enough to look after each other / ourselves.

AUFGABE 10 **Vervollständige die Sätze und benutze *one* oder *ones*.**

I couldn't answer the questions in my last exam because there were only difficult _____ .

This shop sells cheap jeans. I like the black _____ .

There is a French film and a German film on tonight. Let's watch the French _____ .

Anne wants to buy some T-shirts for the summer. She wants a green _____ and two red _____ .

Lucy has got two brothers: An older _____ and a younger _____ .

There is strawberry ice cream and chocolate ice cream for dessert. Which _____ would you prefer?

AUFGABE 11 **Markiere die Fehler in den folgenden Sätzen und korrigiere die Sätze. Ein Satz ist richtig.**

ACHTUNG FEHLER

Sit yourself down and relax.

_____

There is a green apple and a red apple. Which ones would you like?

_____

We met ourselves in the zoo.

_____

My granny is all alone and often talks to herself.

_____

Let's write emails to ourselves.

_____

AUFGABE 12 **Übersetze. Schreibe in dein Übungsheft.**

Was hat sich letzte Nacht ereignet?
Ich muss mir keine Sorgen machen.
Er denkt nur an sich.

Kannst du dich noch erinnern?
Sie duscht jeden Morgen.
Wir müssen uns mehr Zeit geben.

3 Adjektive

3.1 Vergleiche mit Adjektiven

Eine **Gleichheit** wird im Englischen mit der Konstruktion ***as*** **+ Adjektiv +** ***as*** *(genauso ... wie)* ausgedrückt.	Lynn is as tall as Julie. Is New York as big as London?
Eine **Ungleichheit** wird entweder mit der Konstruktion **Komparativ +** ***than*** *(... als)* oder mit ***not as/so ... as*** *(nicht so ... wie)* ausgedrückt. *Aufgepasst:* ***Than*** *(als)* und ***then*** *(dann)* dürfen nicht verwechselt werden!	Windsor Castle is bigger than Buckingham Palace. Living in a city can be more dangerous than living in the country. Sue's car is not as / so fast as Kevin's car. Going by boat is more interesting than going by tube. *Aber:* First we saw the Houses of Parliament, then Tower Bridge.
Ungleichheit kann auch mit ***less ... than*** *(weniger ... als)* ausgedrückt werden. Diese Wendung hat etwa die gleiche Bedeutung wie *not as ... as.*	York is less interesting than (not as interesting as) London.
Mit dem Ausdruck ***the*** **+ Komparativ ...** ***the*** **+ Komparativ** wird im Englischen die deutsche Entsprechung ***je ... desto/umso*** wiedergegeben. *Aufgepasst:* Die Satzstellung ist anders als im Deutschen: Im Englischen lautet sie in beiden Satzteilen **Subjekt + Verb.**	The bigger a car, the more expensive it is. (je größer ...., desto / umso teurer ...) The older Sarah gets, the sillier she becomes. (je älter ..., desto / umso alberner ...) The earlier **I get** up the more tired **I am.** Je früher **ich aufstehe,** desto müder **bin ich.**
Um eine **stetige Steigerung** oder eine allmähliche Entwicklung zum Ausdruck zu bringen, verbindet man im Englischen zwei gleiche Komparativformen mit *and.* Die Wiedergabe im Deutschen erfolgt mit „immer" + Komparativ.	Your English is getting better and better (immer besser). The film got more and more exciting (immer aufregender).

ÜBUNG 1 **Sieh dir die Abbildungen an und vergleiche die Gegenstände mit *as … as*.**

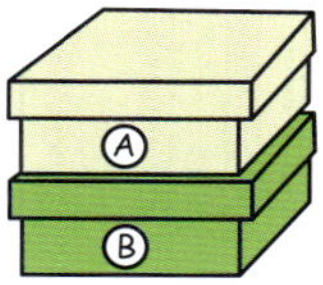

Box A is __________ box B.

Jenny is __________ Liz.

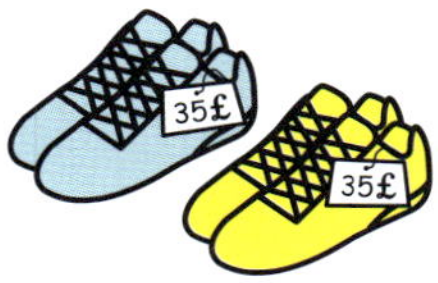

The blue shoes are __________ the yellow ones.

Mrs Miller __________ Mr Jenkins.

ÜBUNG 2 **Formuliere die folgenden Sätze um, indem du *not as … as* benutzt.**

Athens is older than Rome.

Rome isn't as __________ Athens.

My room is bigger than yours.

Your room isn't __________.

You got up earlier than me.

I didn't __________.

We played better than them.

They didn't __________.

I've been here longer than you.

You haven't __________.

Lisa is more nervous than her friend.

Her friend __________.

ÜBUNG 3 **Vervollständige die Sätze mit *as* oder *than*.**

I don't watch TV as much _____ you.

You can eat more sandwiches _____ me.

My mother feels better _____ she felt yesterday.

Jim isn't as clever _____ he thinks.

Switzerland is smaller _____ Germany.

The boys couldn't wait longer _____ an hour.

Is your brother older _____ my brother?

Mexico isn't as big _____ Canada.

ÜBUNG 4 **Vergleiche Jackies Auto mit Amandas Auto mithilfe der Adjektive in den Klammern.**

Amanda's car isn't _____ (big) Jackie's. Jackie's car wasn't _____ (cheap) Amanda's. Jackie's car was _____ (expensive) Amanda's. Amanda's car isn't _____ (modern) Jackie's. Jackie's car is _____ (long) and _____ (wide) Amanda's. Amanda's car isn't _____ (quiet) Jackie's. But Amanda's car is _____ (small) Jackie's, so Amanda's car is _____ (easy) to park in town. Jackie and Amanda both like cars. Jackie is _____ (interested) in cars as Amanda, and she also has _____ (much) time to repair her car herself as Amanda.

ÜBUNG 5 **Übersetze die deutschen Ausdrücke in den Klammern ins Englische.**

Oh dear! You are getting ______ (immer dünner).

______ (je länger) you sleep, ______ (umso müder) you get.

______ (je müder) you are, ______ (desto schwieriger) it is to get up.

The rain was getting ______ (immer schlimmer).

______ (je älter) her son gets, ______ (desto schwieriger) he becomes.

ÜBUNG 6 **Tina hat ihrer Freundin Pat aus Schottland geschrieben. Höre dir Track 3 auf der CD an und vervollständige Tinas Postkarte.**

3

Dear Pat,

Scotland is great, it is ______ (genauso schön wie) ______ Wales. Yesterday, I went climbing. It was ______ (schwieriger als) I thought. We had to climb up very high, but ______ (nicht so hoch wie) Snowdon. I'm going pony trekking with some of the girls at the weekend. I think pony trekking is ______ (mehr Spaß als) mountain biking. The longer I stay, ______ (desto aufregender) it is to be here in Scotland. And the people here are even ______ (freundlicher als) back home in Wales, but the summers here seem to be ______ (genauso kalt) they are in Wales. I hope your holidays aren't ______ (nicht so langweilig wie) they were last year.

Love, Tina

ÜBEN

3.2 Das Adjektiv als Substantiv

Im Gegensatz zum Deutschen können Adjektive im Englischen nicht automatisch als Substantive benutzt werden. Im Singular wird ein zusätzliches Substantiv benötigt.	**Der Blinde** (= der blinde Mann) dort drüben braucht Hilfe. → **The blind man** over there needs help.
Adjektive können im Englischen jedoch als Substantiv verwendet werden, wenn ein ***the*** vorangestellt wird. Sie bezeichnen dann eine **Gruppe** oder eine **Gesamtheit** von Personen:	**Die Blinden** (= blinde Menschen) brauchen die Hilfe von anderen. → **The blind** need the help of other people.
the blind, the rich / the poor, the hungry, the old / the young, the sick, the strong / the weak	The rich of New York (die Reichen / reichen Einwohner New Yorks) met at the mayor's party. Sometimes the young (die Jungen / die jungen Leute) don't understand the older generation. The injured (die Verletzten) are taken to the hospital.
Merke: Das Adjektiv als Substantiv wird wie eine Pluralform verwendet, das heißt, das Verb steht im Plural. Das Adjektiv hat jedoch **kein Plural-*s*.**	The young **are** usually careless. The blind **go** to special schools.
Sind **einzelne** Personen gemeint, so muss das Adjektiv durch ein Substantiv wie *person, man, boy, girl, woman, people* ergänzt werden.	A blind man stood at the side of the road. The sick woman had to go to hospital. Some rich people help the poor. The two young girls were standing at the bus stop.
Einige Adjektive sind **echte Substantive** geworden und kommen im Singular und im Plural vor.	
the black – blacks, the white – whites	There are only a few blacks in this area and they don't talk to the whites.
the individual – individuals *the native – natives*	Must we look after the individuals? The natives had to leave their land.
Sie können eine Gruppe und auch einzelne Personen bezeichnen.	

WISSEN

ÜBUNG 7 **Vervollständige die Sätze mit *the* + Adjektiv (+ Substantiv). Wähle das richtige Adjektiv aus dem Wortspeicher.**

injured – rich – sick – old – young

_______________ have the future in their hands.

There is a home for _______________ in Sally's road.

The ambulance arrived just in time and took _______________ to hospital.

Julia works in hospital. She looks after _______________ .

Robin Hood took the money from _______________ .

ÜBUNG 8 **Übersetze die folgenden Ausdrücke ins Englische. Schreibe sie in dein Übungsheft.**

der Kleine	ein Kranker	die Obdachlosen
die Tote	zwei Schwarze	die Schwachen
der Starke	die Weißen	die Große

ÜBUNG 9 **Vervollständige die Sätze, indem du die richtigen Ausdrücke aus dem Wortspeicher auswählst und übersetzt.**

ein alter Mann – eine reiche Frau – die Armen – ein Blinder – junge Leute

There are some good programmes for _______________ on TV.

There lives _______________ over there in that fantastic huge bungalow.

_______________ was standing at the side of the road with his guide dog.

The car has just hit _______________ who was crossing the street rather slowly.

Many people have no idea of the problems _______________ in big cities have.

Klassenarbeit 1

45 Minuten

AUFGABE 1 **Deine Meinung ist gefragt. Formuliere Vergleiche, indem du die Adjektive in den Klammern benutzt.**

A geography lesson is ______ (good) an English lesson.

Comics are ______ (interesting) books.

Football ______ (popular) tennis.

Hiking ______ (exciting) cycling.

My mother ______ (tall) me.

French ______ (easy) maths.

AUFGABE 2 **„Je …, desto …" – beende die folgenden Sätze.**

The hotter a day, ______ (I / much / drink).

The more words you learn in English, ______ (you / get good / at English).

The more exciting a book, ______ (I / read / long).

The quicker a car, ______ (to be / it / exciting).

The funnier a film, ______ (I / laugh / much).

AUFGABE 3 **Formuliere eine stetige Steigerung. Das Adjektiv in den Klammern hilft dir.**

You couldn't speak French well, but now it is getting ______ (good).

Ben is running. He is getting ______ (quick).

Bread was so cheap, but these days it is getting ______ (expensive).

Houses in big cities are getting ______ (high).

Some streets in my town are getting ______ (dirty).

TESTEN

AUFGABE 4 **Ergänze bei den folgenden Sätzen das Adjektiv in den Klammern mit einem Substantiv, falls dies notwendig ist.**

We should do more for the ______ (poor).

There's a ______ (blind) in our road. She's 16 like me.

The police found a ______ (dead) in the forest.

The two ______ (old) sitting on the park bench live near us.

The ______ (homeless) in London often sleep in the streets.

Some countries have schools for the ______ (rich).

AUFGABE 5 **In jedem der folgenden Sätze ist jeweils ein Fehler. Streiche ihn an und verbessere den Satz, indem du ihn neu schreibst.** ACHTUNG FEHLER

We saw a blind who crossed the street alone.

Julia is a bit taller then me.

You are getting more and more thin.

Do you think the riches are really happy?

His concert was as well as the last one.

The quicker a computer, the most expensive it is.

My bike is older as yours.

The black and the white should live together.

Klassenarbeit 2

45 Minuten

AUFGABE 6 **Vervollständige die Tabelle mit der jeweils richtigen Steigerungsform der Adjektive.**

dark		
	sillier	
		best
intelligent		
	worse	
hot		
		quietest

AUFGABE 7 **Wähle aus dem Wortspeicher das richtige Adjektiv und setze es in der richtigen Steigerungsform mit *than* in die passende Lücke.**

big – tidy – expensive – easy – good – friendly – exciting

The flats in Bond Street are ______ those in Oxford Street. It's amazing what one has to pay there.

Look at my room. It's ______ my brother's. His room looks like a dustbin.

Is London ______ Berlin? – I have no idea, but London has about 7 million people, doesn't it?

Our new neighbours are ______ our old ones. They often look after our cats when we are away on holiday.

Dan thinks German is ______ French. – Well, that's just because he has got an A in German. His German is fantastic. It is definitely ______ his French.

The last Superhero film was ______ the first one. I almost fell asleep when I watched the first Superhero film.

TESTEN

AUFGABE 8 **Bilde mit den folgenden Satzteilen Sätze mit *as ... as*.**

Mr Smart's car / old / Mr Miller's car

Scotland / beautiful / Wales

My grandparents / nice / your grandparents

tennis / popular / football

French / difficult / English

My brother / tall / your brother

AUFGABE 9 **Bilde jeweils Sätze mit den Satzteilen aus der rechten und linken Spalte. Benutze den Superlativ des Adjektivs. Schreibe in dein Übungsheft.**

The Mona Lisa	busy time of the year
Ben Nevis	hot month
Christmas	famous painting in the world
That was	popular tourist attraction in Scotland
July is usually	good meal I have eaten
Loch Ness	high mountain in Great Britain

AUFGABE 10 **Übersetze. Schreibe in dein Übungsheft.**

Die Armen brauchen unsere Hilfe.
Die Reichen leben in dieser Gegend.
Der Kranke wurde ins Krankenhaus gebracht.
Die Jungen wollen nichts mit den Alten zu tun haben.
Die Junge könnte freundlicher sein.
Die Schönen und die Reichen findet man in Los Angeles.

4 Die Zeiten

4.1 Wiederholung: Das *present tense* und das *past tense*

Das *present tense*

Das ***simple present*** steht, wenn etwas regelmäßig, häufig, oft, nie oder auch immer geschieht. **Signalwörter:** *always, never, often, sometimes, usually, on Mondays, every weekend.*	I often **get up** early in the morning. He never **walks** to school. They usually **go** to school by bus.
Es steht ▪ bei Berufen, Hobbys oder typischen Fähigkeiten,	My mother is a vet. John swims in his free time.
▪ bei der Inhaltswiedergabe und aufeinander folgenden Handlungen,	The story is about a young girl. She lives in London. – First he comes home, then he unlocks the door. Finally he watches TV.
▪ bei *when*- und *if*-Sätzen.	If you don't run, you will miss your bus.
Mit dem ***present progressive*** wird eine Handlung beschrieben, die im Augenblick des Sprechens gerade abläuft oder noch nicht abgeschlossen ist. **Signalwörter:** *at the moment, just, now, still, right now.*	Look. It **is raining.** Sally **is** still **reading** a magazine. They **are** just **having** tea. We **are doing** our homework at the moment.
Aufgepasst: Verben der **Sinneswahrnehmung** stehen normalerweise nicht in der Verlaufsform.	The soup tastes good. This song sounds fantastic.

Das *past tense*

Das ***simple past*** beschreibt eine in der Vergangenheit abgeschlossene Handlung. **Signalwörter:** *yesterday, ago,* Zeitangaben mit *last, in 1997.*	She **wrote** a letter. We **went** to the cinema. My friend **had** a party last week. Yesterday we **visited** my grandparents.
Das ***past progressive*** wird verwendet, um ein Ereignis zu beschreiben, das in der Vergangenheit im Verlauf war, als ein neues Ereignis eintrat.	Tom **was doing** his homework when the phone rang. While the Browns **were working** in the garden, it started to rain.

ÜBUNG 1 ***Simple*** **oder** ***progressive?*** **– Unterstreiche die richtige Form des** ***present tense.***

What time do you usually get up / are you usually getting up?

Kim is excited. She is going shopping / goes shopping.

Oh look! It snows / is snowing again.

Jeff is still working / still works on his project in geography.

My parents never eat / are never eating in a restaurant.

Mary sometimes takes / is sometimes taking the dog for a walk.

ÜBUNG 2 **Lies dir die Sätze durch und setze dann das Verb ins** ***simple past.***

Mary often loses her purse. She ______ it last week.

We meet our friends every weekend. We ______ them two weeks ago.

I usually buy some magazines every week. I ______ some last week.

We often go to the cinema on Saturdays. We ______ there yesterday.

My grandparents come to see us every Friday. They ______ to see us last Friday, too.

Mum eats an apple every evening. She ______ one last night, too.

ÜBUNG 3 **Vervollständige die Sätze mit der richtigen Zeitform des Verbs in den Klammern.**

Where's Lisa? – She ______ (still – to write) a letter in her room.

Last week my parents ______ (to fly) to New York.

I ______ (to meet) James in 2008.

She always ______ (to go) to bed at 9:30 p.m.

While the Dicksons were having a garden party, it ______ (to start) to rain heavily.

If you ______ (to do) the washing-up, your mum will be pleased.

Sue and Tim ______ (to lie) on the beach at the moment.

The bus stopped because two children ______ (to run) across the road.

4.2 Das *present perfect*

Das *present perfect simple*

Das *present perfect simple* wird gebildet aus ***have / has + past participle.***	
■ Die **regelmäßigen** Formen des *past participle* enden wie die regelmäßigen Formen des *simple past* auf ***-ed,***	I / you / we / they **have arrived.** He / she / it **has arrived.** He has **worked.** They haven't **stopped.**
■ die **unregelmäßigen** Formen müssen gelernt werden.	She has **written.** We have **gone.**
Das *present perfect simple* wird verwendet, um auszudrücken, dass eine vergangene Handlung noch **Auswirkungen** auf die Gegenwart hat. Es wird auch für Handlungen verwendet, die **gerade erst abgeschlossen** wurden.	I have cut my finger. It hurts. Look, I have bought a new computer. They have opened the windows. The air is fresher now in here. The bus has arrived. Let's get on it.
Die folgenden **Signalwörter** erfordern den Gebrauch des *present perfect simple:* *just – gerade, never – niemals, ever – jemals, so far – bisher, not ... yet – noch nicht, since / for – seit* (↑ nächste Seite)	The guests have just arrived. Have you ever been to London? – No, I have never been there. Jane hasn't done her homework yet.

Das *present perfect progressive*

Das *present perfect progressive* wird gebildet aus ***have / has + been + present participle.***	I / you / we / they **have been waiting.** He / she / it **has been waiting.**
Es drückt aus, dass eine Handlung oder ein Ereignis **in der Vergangenheit begonnen** hat und bis in die Gegenwart **andauert** (und noch länger andauern kann).	I have been running. I'm out of breath now. Sarah has been cooking lunch. The kitchen is still untidy.
Zu den **Signalwörtern** gehören: *how long? – wie lange?, all day – den ganzen Tag, the whole month – den ganzen Monat, for one hour – seit einer Stunde*	How long has she been swimming? – She has been swimming for two hours.

ÜBUNG 4 **Beschreibe, was in den Situationen passiert ist. Wähle aus dem Wortspeicher das richtige Verb und setze es ins *present perfect simple*.**

to take a shower – to tidy their room – to break her arm –
to do the washing-up

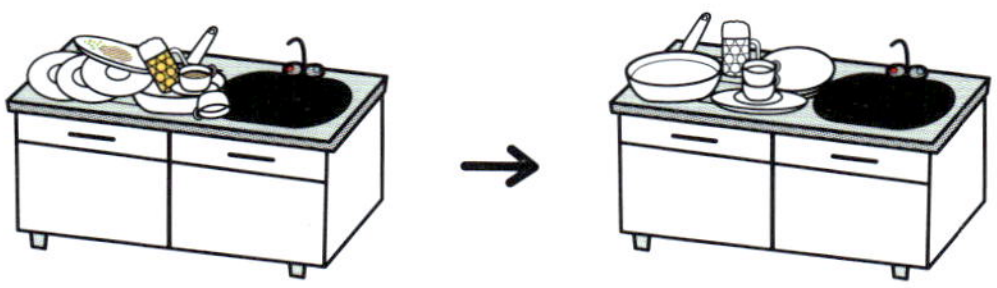

Andy and Kevin ________________ ________________.

Janet ________________ ________________.

Mr Miller ________________ ________________.

Liz and Joe ________________ ________________.

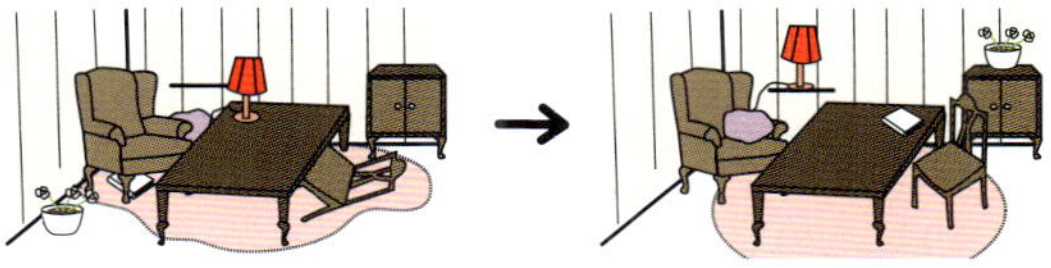

WISSEN

Since* und *for

Since und ***for*** sind Signalwörter, die mit dem ***present perfect*** benutzt werden.

Sie zeigen an, wie lange eine Handlung oder Situation gedauert hat.

Aufgepasst: ***Since*** zeigt den **Zeitpunkt** an, ***for*** die **Zeitspanne.** Die deutsche Bedeutung ist beide Male „seit“.

I have had my computer for two years.
He has been driving since 7 o'clock.
We have been here for two months.
It has been raining since we arrived.

since ten o'clock – since yesterday – since 2008
for three hours – for two days – for a long time

ÜBUNG 5 **Beantworte die folgenden Fragen mithilfe des Verbs und des Signalworts in den Klammern.**

Have you done your homework? – Yes, I ______ (to do – just) it.

Who is that woman? – I don't know. We ______ (to see – never) before.

Has Sue ever been to London? – Yes, she ______ (to be – already) there.

Have the Wilsons organized their party yet? – I think they ______ ______ (to invite – already) their guests.

Where are my keys? – Sorry, but I ______ them ______ (to find – not yet).

Has the train already arrived? – No, it ______ (not to arrive – yet).

ÜBUNG 6 **Vervollständige die Sätze mit *for* oder *since* und setze das Verb in den Klammern in die richtige Form: *present perfect simple* oder *progressive?* Achtung: Manchmal sind beide Formen möglich!**

Jill ______ (to be) at home ______ 5 o'clock.

My grandparents ______ (to live) in England ______ 14 years.

We ______ (to wait) for the bus ______ 20 minutes.

Mr Robertson ______ (not to work) in his office ______ some weeks.

These houses ______ (to be) empty ______ 1998.

Liz ______ (to learn) to play the piano ______ she was six.

Kevin ______ (to have) his bike ______ last Christmas.

Sally ______ (to know) her friend ______ years.

ÜBEN

WISSEN

Präsens im Deutschen, *present perfect* im Englischen

Im Deutschen verwendet man das **Präsens**, wenn man ausdrücken möchte, wie lange etwas schon andauert.

Ich **lese** dieses Buch jetzt schon **seit** einer Woche.

Im Englischen dagegen steht bei *since* und *for* nie das Präsens, sondern das ***present perfect***.

I **have been reading** this book **for** one week now.

ÜBUNG 7 **Formuliere die folgenden Sätze um, indem du *for* oder *since* benutzt. Achte wieder auf die richtige Form – *simple* oder *progressive?***

Susan is in France now. She arrived there four days ago.

She has been in France for four days.

It's raining. It started two hours ago.

It ______ two hours.

Kevin has got a new camera. He bought it in 2009.

He ______ .

Dave plays the guitar. He started when he was eight years old.

______ .

Mr Brown is washing his car. He started to wash it at 4 o'clock.

______ .

ÜBUNG 8 **Setze die Satzteile zu sinnvollen Sätzen zusammen und schreibe sie in dein Übungsheft.**

Andy	hasn't phoned	to Scotland yet.
She	has never stolen	for some days.
My friend	haven't flown	anything in his life.
They	hasn't been to a pub	since last week.
We	have written	six letters so far.

4.3 Das *past perfect*

Das *past perfect simple*

Das *past perfect simple* wird gebildet aus ***had + past participle.*** Für die **regelmäßigen** und **unregelmäßigen** Formen des *past participle* gelten dieselben Regeln wie für die Bildung des *present perfect* (↑ Kap. 4.2).	I / You / We / They **had looked.** He / She / It **had looked.** He **had arrived.** They **hadn't talked.** She **had seen.** We **had thought.**
Das *past perfect simple* steht fast immer in Verbindung mit dem *simple past.* Es wird verwendet, wenn man sich auf einen **Zeitpunkt** bezieht, der sich **vor einem Ereignis im *simple past*** ereignet hat. Es handelt sich also um ein Ereignis, das noch weiter zurückliegt als die Vergangenheit (= Vorvergangenheit).	Laura couldn't buy anything because she **had forgotten** her purse. I arrived at 7:30 but Laura **had** already **left** the bar at 7 o'clock. Roy couldn't find his purse. Maybe someone **had stolen** it.

Das *past perfect progressive*

Das *past perfect progressive* wird gebildet aus ***had + been + present participle.***	I / You / We / They **had been walking.** He / She / It **had been walking.**
Das *past perfect progressive* wird verwendet, wenn (wie beim *past perfect simple*) ein Ereignis vor einem Zeitpunkt in der Vergangenheit stattgefunden hat. Es drückt aus, dass eine Handlung oder ein Zustand in der Vergangenheit **andauerte**, als ein anderes Ereignis einsetzte. Das einsetzende Ereignis steht im *simple past.*	It started to rain. The hikers **had been walking** for quite some time. My bus arrived at 8:45. I **had been waiting** at the bus stop since 8 o'clock.
Wird ein Nebensatz mit ***after*** *(nachdem)* eingeleitet, steht er im *past perfect.* Im Hauptsatz muss das *simple past* stehen. Wird der Nebensatz mit ***when*** *(als)* oder ***before*** *(bevor)* eingeleitet, steht das *simple past.* Im Hauptsatz wird das *past perfect simple / progressive* verwendet.	After Liz had left school *(Nebensatz)*, she went to America *(Hauptsatz).* I had already known Marc *(Hauptsatz)* before I moved to Wales *(Nebensatz).* Tina had been talking to her friend *(Hauptsatz)* when Andy came in *(Nebensatz).*

WISSEN

ÜBUNG 9 **Vervollständige die folgenden Sätze mit der *past perfect simple*-Form des Verbs in den Klammern.**

After we ________ (to buy) the tickets, we went to the concert.

I phoned the police because someone ________ (to steal) my car.

The tourists ________ (to visit) the castle before they went to their hotel.

Kim's classroom was no longer grey. The class ________ (to paint) it green.

John ________ (not to finish) his homework when Peter phoned.

________ you ________ (to go) to Bristol before you flew to London?

ÜBUNG 10 **Die Wilsons wollen nach Cornwall fahren. Schau dir die folgende Bildergeschichte an und formuliere zu jedem Bild einen Satz, der die vorhergehende Handlung nochmals aufgreift. Schreibe in dein Übungsheft.**

1. After the Wilsons had decided to go to Cornwall, they packed their bags.
2. After they had packed ________, they ________.
3. ________, ________ at their hotel.
4. ________, the receptionist ________.
5. … 6. …

ÜBUNG 11 **Mache aus zwei eins: Verbinde die einzelnen Sätze in der angegebenen Reihenfolge mit *after, when* oder *before*.**

Her parents sold their house (1). They bought a bungalow (2).

After her parents had sold their house, they bought a bungalow.

Ben graduated from school (1). He went to university (2).

The lessons began (2). The pupils got to school (1).

The train left (1). They got to the station (2).

The thieves left the bank (1). The police arrived (2).

I started breakfast (1). The doorbell rang (2).

ÜBUNG 12 **Vervollständige die folgenden Sätze, indem du das *simple past* und das *past perfect simple* in jedem Satz verwendest. Beachte die Reihenfolge der Handlung.**

When the ship ______ (to sink), the passengers ______ (to be) at sea for months.

After Anne ______ (to see) a film about King Arthur, she ______ (to want) to read a book about him.

Tim ______ (not to ride) on a horse before he ______ (to spend) a few days on a farm.

When the boys ______ (to arrive) at the café at 12:30, it ______ (to close) half an hour earlier.

The tourists ______ (not to realize) that they ______ (to take) the wrong way.

ÜBEN

ÜBUNG 13 **Höre dir den Text über Cindy auf Track 4 der CD an. Beantworte anschließend die Fragen und achte dabei darauf, dass du die richtige Zeitform wählst.**

4

What language did Cindy learn after she had learnt French?

What did she do when she had learnt Spanish?

What language did she teach after she had taught French?

What did she want to do after she had taught at her school for three years?

What did she do when she had come back home from Madrid?

ÜBUNG 14 **Setze in die Lücken entweder das *past tense*, das *past perfect simple* oder das *past perfect progressive*.**

to live / to move: How long ______ you ______ in Europe before you ______ to New York?

to go: He ______ never ______ by Underground before.

to travel: After he ______ for half an hour he realised that he was going in the wrong direction.

to drive: How long ______ Robert ______ before he had his first accident?

to talk / to hear: My mother ______ to her neighbour when she suddenly ______ a terrible noise.

to collect / to listen / to acquire: Derek ______ Beatles records for a while before he actually ______ to them. He ______ already ______ quite a few records when he decided to sell them.

4.4 Das *simple present* und das *present progressive* zur Wiedergabe der Zukunft

Das *simple present*

Das *simple present* wird zur Wiedergabe der Zukunft verwendet, wenn es sich um einen **feststehenden Termin** handelt, der nicht beeinflussbar ist, wie etwa genaue Zeitangaben, Fahrpläne oder Programme. Deshalb spricht man auch von ***timetable future.***

Das *timetable future* wird vor allem bei folgenden Verben gebraucht:

to arrive, to leave, to begin, to start, to end, to open, to close

Our train leaves at four minutes past twelve.
It arrives in Manchester at twenty to three.
When does the concert start?
The guided tour through London ends at 5 o'clock.
This bookshop closes at 10 p.m.

Das *present progressive*

Das *present progressive* drückt aus, dass jemand etwas für die Zukunft **fest geplant** oder **vereinbart** hat.

What are you doing next week? – I'm meeting Kate in the afternoon, but I'm not doing anything special in the afternoon.
Mum, you needn't collect me after Pete's party. Emma's mother is giving me a lift.

Damit es keine Verwechslungen mit dem *present progressive* zur Wiedergabe von gegenwärtigen Handlungen gibt, werden oftmals Zeitbestimmungen der Zukunft verwendet. Zu diesen **Zeitangaben** gehören:

tomorrow, on Thursday, next week, this summer, every weekend

I'm helping Sarah with her homework. (= Ich helfe ihr gerade.)

Aber: I'm helping Sarah with her homework tomorrow. (= Ich helfe ihr morgen. Es ist vereinbart.)

ÜBUNG 15 **Sieh dir die Termine folgender Personen an und schreibe auf, was sie für die Zukunft geplant haben.**

Tim – visit – his granny – 7:30 p.m.

Paul and Linda – in an hour – play – computer games

Steve – write – letters – tonight

Pam and Ann – tomorrow – go – sports centre – with Ed

ÜBUNG 16 **Mrs Gray, die Lehrerin von Ben, gibt ihrer Klasse die wichtigsten Termine für die Klassenfahrt nach Schottland. Schau dir Mrs Grays Notizen an und vervollständige dann den Text mit der richtigen Form der Zukunft.**

Monday
bus start – 9:30 a.m.
lunch – 12:30 p.m.
arrive Edinburgh – 6 p.m.

Tuesday
Whiskey Museum
guided tour Art Gallery – 2 p.m.

Wednesday
climb Arthur's Seat

Thursday
Holyrood House – 10 a.m.
bus from Youth Hostel – 3 p.m.

Mrs Gray: "Our trip ________ on Monday 3rd. The bus ________ from the main gate at 9:30 a.m. We ________ lunch at 12:30, and the bus ________ in Edinburgh at about 6 o'clock. On Tuesday we ________ the Whiskey Museum with its wonderful exhibition. After that in the afternoon we ________ a guided tour of the Art Gallery. On Wednesday we ________ Arthur's Seat. On Thursday we ________ Holyrood House at 10 a.m. You know that it is a royal palace. Don't forget that the bus ________ from the Youth Hostel at 3 p.m. So don't be late."

Klassenarbeit 1

60 Minuten

AUFGABE 1 **Vervollständige die Sätze, indem du entweder das *present progressive* oder das *simple present* benutzt.**

Sue's grandparents ______ (to live) in Edinburgh.

Listen, Jill! The train ______ (to come)! Hurry up.

My mother ______ (often – to grow) a lot of flowers,

but this year she ______ (not to grow) any.

British pupils ______ (usually – to go) to school in the afternoon.

AUFGABE 2 **Entscheide dich für die richtige Verbform und unterstreiche sie.**

What have you been doing / have you done all afternoon?

Have you done / Have you been doing your homework yet?

John and I have been sitting / have sat in the kitchen all evening.

Sarah hasn't been eating / hasn't eaten anything since lunch.

Someone has stood / has been standing there in the dark for a long time and has watched / has been watching us through the window.

AUFGABE 3 **Bilde Sätze und verwende die richtige Zeit. Das Signalwort hilft dir.**

He – just – to go to the dentist

______

They – to win the World Cup – 2002

______

Some strange people – to try to open the door – at the moment

______

I – not to practise my English vocabulary – yesterday

______

TESTEN

AUFGABE 4 **John blättert gerade in alten Notizen. Schreibe in dein Übungsheft, was er letzte Woche gemacht hat. Achte auf die richtige Form des *past tense!***

holiday – start – on Sunday
the next day – repair my broken bike
on Tuesday – to go to York by bike
later that day – visit the cathedral
when – cycle home – start to rain
get terribly wet – and take a hot bath
while – watch TV – have my tea

AUFGABE 5 **Bilde Fragen und verneinte Antworten. Entscheide, ob du *present perfect simple* oder *present perfect progressive* benötigst.**

Kim / to read / for a long time

Has Kim ?

Kim hasn't .

Alan / to take photos / all afternoon

?

.

Joe / to be / at this school / for five years

?

.

The poor dog / to have / food / for days

?

.

Colin and Fred / to play / tennis / since breakfast

?

.

The Millers / to live / in the North of England / for three years.

?

.

TESTEN

AUFGABE 6 **Lies dir jeweils die Ereignisse durch. Beginne mit dem Satz, der rot markiert ist, und achte auf die richtige Zeitenabfolge in den weiteren Sätzen: *past perfect simple* oder *simple past?***

(1) Somebody broke into the office during night.
(2) We arrived at work in the morning.
(3) We called the police.

We __________ at work in the morning and found that somebody __________ into the office during night. So we __________ the police.

(1) Ann went out.
(2) I tried to phone her this morning.
(3) There was no answer.

I tried to phone Ann this morning but __________ no answer. She __________ out.

(1) Kevin came back from London a few days ago.
(2) I met him the same day.
(3) He looked very well.

I __________ Kevin a few days ago. He __________ well. He __________.

AUFGABE 7 **Setze die richtige Verbform in die Lücke: *past perfect progressive* oder *past perfect simple?***

Sarah and I were good friends. We __________ (to know) each other for a long time.

Mary was sitting on the ground. She was tired. She __________ (to run).

When I arrived, everybody was sitting round the table and talking. They __________ (already – to eat).

Sue was sad when she sold her bike. She __________ (to have) it for a very long time.

When I arrived, Kate __________ (already – to wait) for me.

Klassenarbeit 2

45 Minuten

AUFGABE 8 **Das *present tense* oder das *past tense?* Unterstreiche in den folgenden Sätzen die richtige Form.**

My friend Sally is going / went / goes to New York last year.

Grandfather broke his arm while he was cycling / cycled / cycles home.

When I see / saw / was seeing him, he was carrying a gun.

Who comes / is coming / was coming to Jane's party next week?

Bill is an architect. He enjoys / is enjoying / enjoyed his job.

What does / is / did Anne do / doing / do? I think she is working in the garden.

AUFGABE 9 **Beantworte die folgenden Fragen in der jeweils richtigen Zeitform. Verwende in der Antwort das Verb in der Klammer.**

What has Jane just done? She (to write letters) .

What did you do last weekend? I (to go shopping) .

What have the Millers been doing all morning? They (to play tennis) .

What was Harry doing between 7 o'clock and 8 o'clock? He (to phone a friend) .

What have Philip and Nick already done? They (to take the dogs for a walk) .

AUFGABE 10 **Bilde aus den folgenden Satzteilen Sätze. Achte darauf, dass du den Infinitiv des Verbs in die richtige Zeit setzt – das Signalwort in der Klammer hilft dir dabei. Schreibe in dein Übungsheft.**

Pete's mum / to cook / Spanish food (since she was a child)
Sam / to teach German (in 1997)
Her friend / to be ill (for three days)
His parents / to live / Brighton / to live in Oxford (after)
Bob / to play / for Manchester United (from March to June)
We / to leave for France (tomorrow)
The pupils / to study / in the library (at the moment)
Mary / to wash her hair / to go to the cinema with Nick (before)

AUFGABE 11 **Bringe die passenden Satzhälften zusammen – die Signalwörter helfen dir dabei – und schreibe hinter jeden Satz die Zeitform des Verbs.**

He flew in a helicopter	for two hours now.
My aunt was making sandwiches	yet.
Mike was a dancer	since yesterday.
My friends have been watching TV	last summer.
Their daughter hasn't learned to swim	from 2004 to 2008.
My dog has been lying under my bed	while she was listening to the radio.

He flew in a helicopter last summer. (simple past)

AUFGABE 12 **Übersetze die Sätze ins Englische.**

Bevor wir Rita ins Krankenhaus gebracht haben, ist sie vom Rad gefallen.

Es regnet. Zieh deine Gummistiefel *(wellies)* an.

Tom ist bisher schon zwei Mal umgezogen.

Sie hört sich manchmal die alten Schallplatten an.

Sue und Jim sitzen immer noch am Computer.

Klassenarbeit 3

45 Minuten

AUFGABE 13 **Bei der folgenden Aufgabe sind die Zeiten und Verben durcheinander geraten. Setze die unterstrichenen Verbformen in den jeweils passenden Satz. Schreibe in dein Übungsheft.**

ACHTUNG FEHLER

I was running to Switzerland yet.
My train watched at 7:30 a.m.
The children haven't been a DVD two hours ago.
Hey look! Mrs Green's cat leaves next to the pond.
Chris is sitting through the park last Sunday morning.

AUFGABE 14 **Schreibe mithilfe der Satzteile in den Wortspeichern einen kleinen Text über Liz in dein Übungsheft. Aufgepasst: Du musst das *present perfect* und das *past perfect* jeweils in der *simple*- oder *progressive*-Form verwenden!**

live – Manchester – since 2007 / live in England all her life / meet – best friends – Sandra – Jill – Dave – when – join Park School / that means – she – know them – seven years

after – she – come to Manchester – she – start to play football / she – play football – for some years now

she – have a penfriend from Germany – for three years / they – write a lot / her penfriend – promise to visit her – but – not visit her yet

AUFGABE 15 **Überprüfe, ob du das *present perfect* und das *past perfect* richtig einsetzen kannst. Achte auf die richtige Übersetzung von „seit“! Schreibe in dein Übungsheft.**

1. Andrew lernt seit den letzten Sommerferien Deutsch.
   Bevor Andrew Deutsch gelernt hat, sprach er schon Französisch.
2. Wie lange wohnt ihr schon in eurem neuen Haus?
   Wir wohnen seit einem Monat in diesem Haus.
   Bevor wir in dieses Haus gezogen waren, hatten wir eine Mietswohnung.
3. Unsere Mannschaft hat noch kein Spiel verloren.
   Nachdem wir letztes Jahr einige Spiele verloren hatten, übten wir mehr.
4. Wie lange wart ihr unterwegs gewesen *(to be on the road)*?
   Als wir endlich ankamen, waren wir seit mehr als fünf Stunden gefahren.

Modale Hilfsverben

5.1 *Dürfen*

may / might / mustn't

May und ***might*** werden benutzt, um ■ höflich um Erlaubnis zu bitten, ■ Erlaubnis zu geben, ■ über mögliche Handlungen zu spekulieren.	May / might I ask a question? You may / might sit down. I may / might visit you tomorrow.
Might ist noch höflicher als *may*.	
May not und ***mustn't*** bringen ein **Verbot** zum Ausdruck. *May not* ist höflicher als *mustn't*.	You mustn't / may not make too much noise. You mustn't / may not smoke in here.
Achtung: Zwischen *must* und *to have got to* gibt es einen Bedeutungsunterschied: *Must* drückt ein **persönliches Bedürfnis** aus, *to have got to* bezeichnet einen **äußeren Zwang.**	I am thirsty. I must drink something. I have got to do the washing-up. My parents told me to.

to be allowed to

May / must / mustn't können nur im *present tense* verwendet werden.	
In den fehlenden Zeitformen verwendet man für ***may / might / mustn't*** die **Ersatzform *to be allowed to.*** *To be allowed to* kann in allen Zeiten, auch im *present tense,* stehen.	They were allowed to sit down. You haven't been allowed to make too much noise. We will be allowed to take some pictures. Are we allowed to take our own drinks?
Aufgepasst: Das unpersönliche „Es ist verboten, etwas zu tun" oder „Es ist nicht erlaubt, etwas zu tun" kann nicht wörtlich übersetzt werden. Im Englischen verwendet man die persönliche Konstruktion ***you are (not) allowed to do something.***	You are not allowed to smoke in here. (= Es ist verboten, hier zu rauchen.) You were not allowed to cross the street here. (= Es war verboten, die Straße hier zu überqueren.)

ÜBUNG 1 **Formuliere zu den folgenden Sätzen Fragen, in denen der Sprecher um Erlaubnis bittet.**

Sarah wants to open the window.

Sarah: " ?"

The pupil wants to ask a question.

Pupil: " ?"

Mr Miller wants to sit down.

Mr Miller: " ?"

Mary and John want to have another cup of tea.

Mary and John: " ?"

ÜBUNG 2 **Sieh dir die Hausordnung der Jugendherberge an, in der Matt seine Ferien verbracht hat. Schreibe in dein Übungsheft, was Matt tun und nicht tun durfte.**

Beispiel: Matt was allowed to ...

HOUSE RULES

No parties!

No music after 9 p.m.!

Showers every day!

Use washing-machine once a week!

Make hot drinks in the kitchen!

No smoking!

ÜBUNG 3 **Unterstreiche das richtige Hilfsverb.**

Jane might / was allowed to go out tomorrow.

May / Must I have another sandwich?

My parents were allowed to / may park their car in front of the hotel yesterday.

Visitors might / mustn't feed the animals. They are not allowed to feed them.

When you are 18, you will be allowed to / have been allowed to drive a car.

Sue was allowed to / may use the telephone when she was at the Brown's.

Students mustn't / might use their mobile phones in class. It's a house rule.

5.2 *Müssen* und *sollen*

must und *needn't*

Must und ***needn't*** werden benutzt, um auszudrücken, dass man ■ etwas für notwendig oder für nicht notwendig hält, ■ jemanden zu etwas auffordern will.	We must leave now. You needn't write the text again. You must come and visit us.
Must und *needn't* können nur im *present tense* verwendet werden. In den fehlenden Zeitformen verwendet man ■ für ***must*** die **Ersatzform *to have to,*** ■ für ***needn't*** die **Ersatzform *not to have to.***	Did he have to wait long? We had to book seats. She didn't have to change trains. They will have to get up early. Sarah won't have to work so much next time.
To have to / not to have to kann in allen Zeitformen, auch im *present tense,* stehen.	I have to pay for my drinks. They haven't had to paint their room so far.
To have to wird häufiger gebraucht als ***must,*** vor allem im amerikanischen Englisch. Im britischen Englisch ist auch ***to have got to*** gebräuchlich, allerdings nur im *present tense.*	When do you have to leave tomorrow? I have (got) to leave pretty early.

shall und *should*

Shall wird verwendet, um ■ einen Wunsch zu erfragen oder ■ einen Vorschlag zu machen.	Shall I make us something to eat? Shall I open the window? Shall we have lunch now?
Should / shouldn't wird verwendet, um ■ einen Ratschlag zu erteilen oder ■ eine Verpflichtung zum Ausdruck zu bringen.	Tom is tired. He shouldn't stay up late. Liz should do her homework.
Should kann auch in *that*-Sätzen stehen, um eine persönliche Stellungnahme auszudrücken. In diesem Fall wird es nicht mit „sollte" wiedergegeben.	It's the best that the girls should sleep on the first floor. (= Es ist am besten, wenn die Mädchen im ersten Stock schlafen.)

ÜBUNG 4 **Vervollständige die folgenden Sätze mit den Verben im Wortspeicher, indem du eine Notwendigkeit zum Ausdruck bringst.**

to go – to wear – to pass – to get up

My eyes are not very good. I ______ glasses.

Sam has got a terrible toothache. He ______ to a dentist.

Jill starts work at 7 o'clock. She ______ early every morning.

Before you get your report, you ______ your exams.

ÜBUNG 5 **Formuliere die folgenden Vorschläge um, indem du *shall* benutzt.**

Let's go for a walk. → Shall we go for a walk?

I can open the window. → ______ ?

Let's have something to eat. → ______ ?

I can answer the phone. → ______ ?

ÜBUNG 6 **Lies die folgenden Fragen und bringe zum Ausdruck, dass das, was die Personen tun, nicht notwendig ist. Achte auf die richtige Zeit.**

Why are you going outside? You don't have to go outside.

Why were Simon and Peter waiting? They ______ .

Why will you get up early? You ______ so early.

Why is your father working so hard? He ______ so hard.

Why will you go by train? You ______ by train.

WISSEN +

Die Ersatzformen für *can – können*

Wird mit *can* eine Fähigkeit ausgedrückt, benutzt man die Ersatzform ***to be able to***.

He can drive. → He is able to drive.

Ist mit *can* eine Erlaubnis gemeint, steht die Ersatzform ***to be allowed to***.

You can stay up late. → You are allowed to stay up late.

ÜBUNG 7 **Vervollständige die folgenden Fragen. Achte wieder auf die richtige Zeit!**

I have to get up early tomorrow. → What time ______ ?

Tina had to wait a long time. → How long ______ ?

We had to move house. → Why ______ ?

My parents will have to buy a new car. → Why ______ ?

Jane hasn't had to hand in her homework yet. → Why ______ ?

Mary has to make breakfast every morning. → When ______ ?

ÜBUNG 8 **Höre dir Track 5 auf der CD an und vervollständige die folgenden Sätze. Achte dabei immer auf das richtige modale Hilfsverb.**

5

We don't have anything to eat in the fridge so ______ .

I'm terribly late. I ______ .

It's late. I think we ______ .

If it rains tomorrow, the children ______ I'll take them to school.

James put on weight. The doctor thinks he ______ .

This car is too expensive. Mr Hill ______ .

It's an exciting book. You ______ .

These shoes are too big for you. I don't think ______ .

ÜBEN

ÜBUNG 9 **Sieh dir die folgenden Bilder an und schreibe auf, was du über die jeweiligen Personen sagen würdest.**

John ______________________________.

Mary ______________________________.

Mrs Miller ______________________________.

Mr Taylor ______________________________.

ÜBUNG 10 **Übersetze die folgenden Sätze ins Englische. Achte besonders auf die richtige Übersetzung von *müssen* und *sollen!***

Mein Fahrrad ist schmutzig. Ich muss es putzen.

Wo sollen wir dieses Jahr Urlaub machen?

Du solltest mehr Sport machen.

Sollen wir uns um 19.30 Uhr treffen?

Musst du früh ins Bett?

Musstet ihr gestern lange vor dem Kino warten?

Klassenarbeit 1

60 Minuten

AUFGABE 1 **Setze die Modalverben aus dem Wortspeicher in den folgenden Text ein. Jedes Verb soll nur einmal benutzt werden.**

should – mustn't – might – must – shall – needn't

You ______ use your mobile phone in class.

Look at those clouds! It looks like it ______ rain.

Lucy's room is untidy, so she ______ tidy it up.

My jeans are clean, Mum. You ______ wash them.

My father ______ get up very early every morning.

Frances, ______ we meet at the Internet café in High Street?

AUFGABE 2 **Schaue dir die folgenden Bilder an und entscheide, was die jeweiligen Personen (nicht) dürfen, (nicht) müssen oder (nicht) sollen.**

Charlie ______
______.

You ______
______.

The two girls ______
______.

John ______
______.

TESTEN

AUFGABE 3 **Was dürfen, müssen oder sollen die Personen tun oder nicht tun? Lies dir die Sätze durch und entscheide dich dann für das richtige Modalverb.**

Kim is watching an old lady who is carrying some heavy bags of shopping.

Kim ______ (to help).

You walk past a snack bar with your friend. You are hungry and the sausages smell good. You say: " ______ (to eat)?"

Sue and Allan are always late for the bus. They ______ (to get up earlier).

You mustn't feed the tigers at the zoo. They ______ (to bite) you.

Sally's mother has already made Sally's bed. So Sally ______ (to make it).

George met a nice girl at the disco last night. He gave her his phone number.

The girl ______ (to phone).

AUFGABE 4 **Ergänze die folgenden Sätze mit Modalverben. Die roten Signalwörter helfen dir, die richtige Zeit zu finden. Achtung: Manchmal brauchst du auch die verneinte Form des modalen Hilfsverbs!**

Julie ______ do her homework twice yesterday because she had made too many mistakes.

If you enter this palace, you ______ take photos, but you can buy some postcards in the shop outside the palace.

Jessica cut herself last night, but she ______ go to the doctor's.

Pupils ______ use their dictionaries so far. They will surely be allowed to use them next time.

Mr Evans ______ take a taxi tomorrow because he has an important meeting.

TESTEN

AUFGABE 5 **Durch welche Verbote, Ratschläge, Verpflichtungen oder Aufforderungen wird dein Leben bestimmt? Schreibe zu den Hinweisen Sätze über dich, indem du das richtige Modalverb wählst.**

usually / at school: I

yesterday / my mother in the kitchen:

next week / to stay the night:

not yet / disco:

sometimes / my room:

every evening / the news:

next summer / holiday:

when I was ten:

AUFGABE 6 **Übersetze die folgenden Sätze ins Englische und schreibe sie in dein Übungsheft. Achte auf das richtige Modalverb und die richtige Zeit!**

Ben, sollen wir schwimmen gehen?
Wann durftest du zum ersten Mal auf eine Party gehen?
Justin sollte nicht so viel Schokolade essen.
Am Wochenende werde ich vielleicht Sue treffen.
Musstest du letzte Woche deinem Vater im Garten helfen?
Tinas Eltern sollten versuchen, ihre Tochter zu verstehen.
Wir brauchten die Küche nicht zu streichen.

Das Passiv

6.1 Das Passiv im *simple present* und *present progressive*

Verwendung des Passivs

Das Passiv *(passive voice)* stellt eine Handlung aus einer anderen Sicht dar: Es betont, *was* gemacht wird, d. h. die Handlung selbst ist wichtig und nicht die Person, die die Handlung ausführt.

In einem **Aktivsatz** führt das Subjekt eine Handlung aus.

A policeman **stops** the traffic every morning.

In einem **Passivsatz** geschieht etwas mit dem Subjekt.

The traffic **is stopped** every morning.

Bildung des Passivs

Das Passiv wird immer mit einer Form von ***to be*** und dem ***past participle*** gebildet. Die Form von *to be* wird wie beim Aktiv in die jeweilige Personalform gesetzt.

Das Passiv im ***simple present*** wird also wie folgt gebildet:

is / are + past participle

A letter is written every day.
A movie is watched every weekend.
Our car is often checked.
Houses aren't built every year.
Games are usually played in the evening.

Das Passiv im ***present progressive*** wird so gebildet:

is / are being + past participle

A letter is being written at the moment.
A movie is being watched now.
Our car is just being checked.
Houses aren't being built at the moment.
Look! Games are being played.

ÜBUNG 1 **Bilde aus den Satzteilen Sätze im *simple present* des Passivs.**

the office / to clean / every day

this room / not to use / very often

crisps / to eat / on Saturday evenings

stories / not to read / every weekend

ÜBUNG 2 **Bilde Sätze im *present progressive* des Passivs.**

my room / to clean / now

cheap books / to sell / in front of that shop over there

Sally's house / to paint / at the moment

a new bridge / just / to build

ÜBUNG 3 **Sieh dir die Bilder an. Was passiert gerade? Benutze die richtige Passivform.**

The car ______ .

The windows ______ .

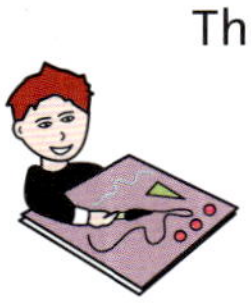

A picture ______ .

ÜBUNG 4 **Vervollständige den folgenden Text mit der korrekten Passivform. Achte auf die richtige Zeit!**

In Switzerland four languages ______ (to speak).

Do you know when the post ______ (usually – to collect)?

Look, Kevin! Your bed ______ (to make) again.

Their bins ______ (always – to empty) in the evening.

It is 6 p.m. – the bins ______ (to empty) now.

A lot of fruit and vegetables ______ (to grow) here.

The grass ______ (to cut) at the moment.

The fire alarm at our school ______ (to test) every month.

ÜBUNG 5 **Verwandle die Aktivsätze in Passivsätze. Schreibe sie in dein Übungsheft.**

Someone is taking John's dog for a walk.
Somebody is painting the door.
My mother does the washing-up every afternoon.
Somebody often drops rubbish in the playground.
Does anyone speak English in this shop? Nobody speaks English in here.
Drivers sometimes break the speed limit.
Mum isn't making my breakfast today.

WISSEN +

Passivsätze mit dem *by-agent*
In Passivsätzen wird der **Verursacher** einer Handlung oftmals nicht erwähnt. Wenn er aber genannt werden soll, so verwendet man den ***by-agent.***

Janet never invites Jack to her parties. → Jack is never invited **by Janet** to her parties.

Er entspricht dem Subjekt des Aktivsatzes und betont, wer oder was etwas verursacht hat.

The fire brigade is rescuing an old woman. → An old woman is being rescued **by the fire brigade.**

Aufgepasst: Der *by-agent* steht meistens am Ende des Satzes.

The pupils greeted the teacher. → The teacher was greeted **by the pupils.**

ÜBUNG 6 **Korrigiere die rot markierten Satzteile, sodass die Sätze inhaltlich richtig sind.**

Planes are flown by taxi-drivers.

Nonsense. Planes are flown ______.

Bread is made by butchers.

That's wrong. Bread ______.

Patients are examined by vets.

Rubbish. ______.

Thieves are caught by nurses.

Of course not. ______.

ÜBUNG 7 **Bilde Passivsätze mit dem *by-agent* und schreibe sie in dein Übungsheft.**

English pupils / French / often / to learn
these stamps / to collect / my parents
at the moment / this hit CD / to make / Joss Stone
to present / these paintings / the Queen / every summer

ÜBUNG 8 **Wähle aus dem Wortspeicher den richtigen *by-agent.***

a heavy storm – a famous pop star – a reporter – Inspector Baxter – our headmistress Mrs Jennings

The parents are usually welcomed by ______.

Many visitors are being interviewed ______.

The kidnapper is being questioned ______.

The houses are being damaged ______.

These songs are sometimes sung ______.

ÜBUNG 9 **Übersetze und schreibe die Sätze in dein Übungsheft.**

Die Straßen werden jeden Tag gereinigt.
Das Haus wird gerade abgerissen.
Schau! Es werden gerade zwei Männer von der Polizei festgenommen.
Meine Eltern werden jeden Monat von unseren Nachbarn eingeladen.

ÜBEN

6.2 Das Passiv bei Verben mit Präpositionen

Verben mit Präpositionen

Das Passiv kann auch von Verben gebildet werden, die mit einer **Präposition** *(preposition)* verbunden sind, z. B.:

to break into – einbrechen
to look after – sich kümmern um
to talk about – sprechen über
to think of – denken an

Someone is breaking into the shop over there. → The shop over there is being broken into.
Our neighbour usually looks after my daughter. → My daughter is usually looked after by our neighbour.
The class often talks about English history. → English history is often talked about.
They usually think of everything. → Everything is usually thought of.

Verb und Präposition gehören im Englischen so eng zusammen, dass sie auch im Passivsatz **nicht getrennt** werden. So ergibt sich bei Passivsätzen mit Verb und Präposition folgende Satzstellung:

Subjekt + Verb + Präposition + Objekt *(+ by-agent)*

Feststehende Ausdrücke

Es gibt eine Reihe von feststehenden Ausdrücken, die aus **Verb + Objekt + Präposition** bestehen:

to make fun of – sich lustig machen über
to pay attention to – achten auf
to take care of – sich kümmern um
to take notice of – beachten
to feel sorry for – bemitleiden

Simon sometimes makes fun of his sister. → His sister is sometimes made fun of by Simon.
Sarah isn't paying attention to Mrs Adams. → Mrs Adams isn't being paid attention to by Sarah.
My parents take care of Aunt Kate's dog every summer. → Aunt Kate's dog is taken care of by my parents every summer.
Jill often feels sorry for her sick friend. → Jill's sick friend is often felt sorry for by Jill.

Auch hier steht die Präposition im Passivsatz immer unmittelbar nach dem Substantiv:

Subjekt + Verb + Objekt + Präposition *(+ by-agent)*

ÜBUNG 10 **In den folgenden Passivsätzen ist die Präposition an die falsche Stelle gerutscht. Schreibe die Sätze neu in dein Übungsheft und achte dabei auf die richtige Satzstellung!**

The problem is being talked by the group about.
A lot of old houses are being down pulled at the moment.
The key is often for looked by Sue.
These signs are of never taken notice by many tourists.

ÜBUNG 11 **Bringe die Satzteile dieser Passivsätze in die richtige Reihenfolge.**

are being at by many visitors looked these pictures

by two men the Millers' house into is being broken

always for my drinks are paid

to Kim is being talked by some boys at the moment

our neighbour's daughter after my baby brother looked by often is

spoken to we by a lot of tourists are being

ÜBUNG 12 **Verwandle die Aktivsätze in Passivsätze. Achte auf die Präposition und vergiss nicht den *by-agent!* Schreibe die Sätze in dein Übungsheft.**

Beispiel: Tom often thinks about this project.
→ This project is often thought about by Tom.

My brother often gives away his CDs.
Mr Jenkins is putting a lot of time into his work.
Mary often takes care of Mrs Baxter's cat.
Timmy is taking off his pullover.
This music often reminds Sue of her last holiday.

ÜBEN

WISSEN +

Das unpersönliche Passiv
Das unpersönliche Passiv wird oft in Zeitungsartikeln eingesetzt, wenn eine Information nicht gesichert ist. Es wird gebildet aus *it* + *is* + *past participle* + *that*. Häufig steht es mit *said, thought, reported* und *known*.

It is reported that the president is quite ill. **It is said that** four people were hurt.

ÜBUNG 13 **Bilde Passivsätze mit Präpositionen. Achte auf die Verwendung der richtigen Zeit! Schreibe in dein Übungsheft.**

The new cars	to take care of	every summer
The boys	to laugh at	at the moment
Her friends	to pull down	now
The dogs	to talk about	always
This bridge	to ask out	every weekend
The new books	to look at	by a lot of people

ÜBUNG 14 **Übersetze die deutschen Wörter in den Klammern ins Englische.**

The tape (wird gerade angehört) ______ by the students.

These exciting stories about Robin Hood (werden oft vorgelesen, *to read out*) ______ by our teacher.

The sofa (wird gerade abgestellt) ______ in the Dixon's living room.

This back room (wird aufgebrochen) ______ almost twice a month.

Hope (wird niemals aufgegeben) ______.

Tony has broken his arm. He (wird bedauert) ______ by all his friends.

6.3 Das Passiv bei Verben mit zwei Objekten

Einige Verben benötigen **zwei Objekte:** ein *direktes* und ein indirektes Objekt. Zu ihnen gehören:	
to give, to offer, to promise, to show, to sell, to send, to tell	They usually give the children (= indirektes Objekt) *the largest room* (= direktes Objekt). My grandma is telling me *an adventure story.* My mum often offers me *sweets.*
Passivsätze mit Verben und zwei Objekten können auf zwei Arten gebildet werden: ■ das indirekte Objekt eines Aktivsatzes (= die Person) wird zum **Subjekt** des Passivsatzes,	Aktiv: My mum often offers me („wem?") sweets. Passiv: **I** am often offered sweets by my mum.
■ das *direkte Objekt* (= Sachobjekt) eines Aktivsatzes wird zum **Subjekt** eines Passivsatzes.	Aktiv: My mum often offers me *sweets* („wen oder was?"). Passiv: **Sweets** are often offered to me by my mum.
Aufgepasst: Wird das indirekte Objekt zum Subjekt im Passivsatz, muss das Pronomen verändert werden: me → I us → we him → he them → they her → she	The woman is showing **me** some jeans. → **I** am being shown some jeans. John's father gives **him** his pocket money every Sunday. → **He** is given his pocket money every Sunday.
You bleibt gleich.	I give **you** a book. → **You** are given a book by me.
Entspricht das Subjekt des Passivsatzes dem **indirekten Objekt** des Aktivsatzes, so nennt man diese Passivform **„persönliches Passiv"**, weil es sich dabei meist um eine Person handelt. Bei der Übersetzung ins Deutsche wird größtenteils *man* oder *jemand* verwendet.	I have been given some details about holidays in Scotland. (Man hat mir einige Details über Ferien in Schottland gegeben.) The tourists are being shown the way to the cathedral. (Jemand zeigt den Touristen den Weg zur Kathedrale.)

ÜBUNG 15 **Finde zu den folgenden Passivsätzen die zweite Möglichkeit, um das Passiv mit zwei Objekten zu bilden.**

Our dog is usually given a dog biscuit in the evening.

A dog biscuit is usually given to our dog in the evening.

The guests are just being offered coffee.

I am often told silly stories.

Every lesson new English exercises are given to us.

They are being told some important information.

A new bike is usually promised Pete before his birthday.

ÜBUNG 16 **Setze die folgenden Sätze ins Passiv. Benutze das persönliche Passiv.**

My parents give me my pocket money every month.

I am given my pocket money by my parents every month.

Tim never tells us funny jokes.

The guide is showing the tourists the most interesting sights.

John's friends never offer him a cigarette.

Every summer Pat sends her penfriend a long letter.

Klassenarbeit 1

45 Minuten

AUFGABE 1 **Lies dir die folgenden Sätze durch und entscheide, ob es sich um einen Aktiv- oder um einen Passivsatz handelt.**

	aktiv	passiv
A lot of vegetables are grown here.	☐	☐
The post is usually collected at 12 o'clock.	☐	☐
This company makes a lot of new computers.	☐	☐
Mrs Dodson phones her mother every day.	☐	☐
The living room is being painted by Luke's father.	☐	☐
Sue is tidying her room at the moment.	☐	☐
A lot of airports are being build just now.	☐	☐
I am woken by my father every morning.	☐	☐

AUFGABE 2 **Sieh dir die Bilder an und schreibe zu jedem Bild einen Passivsatz, in dem du das *present progressive* benutzt.**

1.

2.

3.

4.

1. The park ____________________.
2. The shop ____________________.
3. A horror film ____________________.
4. An exam ____________________.

TESTEN

AUFGABE 3 **Wandle die Passivsätze aus der vorangegangenen Übung ins *simple present* des Passivs um. Wähle für jeden Satz ein Signalwort aus dem Wortspeicher und schreibe die vollständigen Sätze in dein Übungsheft.**

every day – every weekend – sometimes – every week

AUFGABE 4 **Setze die folgenden Sätze ins Passiv. Verwende keinen *by-agent*.**

People don't use this road very often.

How do we learn foreign languages?

Someone is giving little Timmy a toy trumpet.

Why do people often break into that supermarket?

Somebody is following our car.

Somebody sends Ann a parcel every month.

AUFGABE 5 **Übersetze die folgenden Sätze ins Englische und schreibe sie in dein Übungsheft.**

Ich werde immer von meiner Mutter geweckt.
Wo werden die Süßigkeiten aufbewahrt?
Man kümmert sich jeden Tag um die kranken Menschen.
Man bietet einem Freund immer etwas zu trinken an.
Wann wirst du von deinen Eltern von der Schule abgeholt *(to collect)*?
Englisch wird auf der ganzen Welt verstanden.

Klassenarbeit 2

45 Minuten

AUFGABE 6 **Wähle das richtige Verb aus dem Wortspeicher und setze es im Passiv in die Sätze ein. Wähle das *simple present*.**

to cut down – to encourage – to take – to speak – to pollute – to visit

The water ________ by chemicals.

Injured people ________ to hospitals by ambulances.

Sometimes trees ________ in forests.

English ________ in Ireland.

London ________ by many tourists every year.

Pupils all over the world ________ to learn foreign languages.

AUFGABE 7 **Vervollständige den folgenden Text mit den korrekten Passiv- oder Aktivformen. Achte auf die richtige Zeitform.**

Sign ________ in two languages in Wales. (to write)

Every morning Mrs Clark ________ our homework. (to collect)

Lost things ________ to the tourist information centre. (to take)

This film ________ at the moment. (not to show)

We ________ food into a fridge to keep it fresh. (to put)

Today food ________ by the chef only. (to cook)

Lunch ________ on Mondays at this restaurant. (not to serve)

Many people ________ in road accidents every year. (to die)

AUFGABE 8 **Verwandle die Sätze entweder in Aktivsätze oder Passivsätze. Achte bei den Passivsätzen darauf, ob du einen *by-agent* benötigst. Schreibe in dein Übungsheft.**

This shop here sells cars.
They are offering haggis to the tourists.
Some pupils are taught Spanish by teachers at this school.
Pete is tidying his room.
When do people celebrate Valentine's Day?
What is being done by us to help them?

AUFGABE 9 **Ergänze die Sätze mithilfe des Wortspeichers. Achte darauf, dass die Verben im Passiv eine Präposition benötigen. Wähle als Zeitform das *simple present*.**

to laugh – to think – to talk – to look – to pay – to write

for – about – after – to – of – at

Sick people by nurses and doctors.

We by our company.

During the party all kinds of activities .

Funny persons .

She by her parents.

This famous star by a lot of magazines.

AUFGABE 10 **Übersetze die folgenden Sätze ins Englische. Achtung: Die Verben haben zwei Objekte! Vergiss den *by-agent* nicht, falls dieser notwendig ist.**

Den Schülern wird gerade von ihrer Lehrerin viele Hausaufgaben gegeben.

Den Arbeitern wird gewöhnlich viel Geld bezahlt.

Das alte Haus wird gerade von unseren Großeltern an eine junge Familie verkauft.

Die Welpen *(puppies)* werden mir von meinem Nachbarn gezeigt.

Meine Freunde bekommen manchmal von mir kleine Geschenke.

AUFGABE 11 **Finde zu allen Sätzen aus Aufgabe 10 eine zweite Möglichkeit des Passivsatzes. Schreibe in dein Übungsheft.**

7 Der Satz

7.1 Bedingungssätze

Ein Bedingungssatz besteht aus einem *if*-Satz und einem Hauptsatz. Der ***if*-Satz** beschreibt die **Bedingung**, der **Hauptsatz** drückt die tatsächlichen oder möglichen **Folgen** aus.

If we hurry (*if*-Satz), we will catch the bus (Hauptsatz).
We could have gone swimming (Hauptsatz) if you had come earlier (*if*-Satz).

Bedingungssatz Typ I

Der Bedingungssatz Typ I drückt eine Bedingung aus, die der Sprecher für realistisch, also für **erfüllbar** hält.

If Pat calls this evening (falls sie anruft), I will ask her to supper.
You will get your flight cheaper if you book your flight earlier (falls du früher buchst).

Die Bedingung im ***if*-Satz** steht im ***simple present***, die Folge im **Hauptsatz** steht im ***will-future***.

Neben dem *will-future* können im Hauptsatz auch *can / must* + Infinitiv oder der Imperativ auftreten.

If Janet has time, she can help you with your homework.
Don't shout if you are scared.

Bedingungssatz Typ II

Der Bedingungssatz Typ II wird verwendet, wenn man eine Bedingung für unrealistisch, also **nicht erfüllbar** hält.

Die Bedingung im ***if*-Satz** steht im ***past tense***, die Folge im **Hauptsatz** im ***conditional I*** (*would / might / could* + Infinitiv).

Nach *I / he / she / it* kann statt *was* auch *were* verwendet werden.

If I had a lot of money (habe ich aber nicht), I would go on a world tour.
Pam could go out more if she earned more (sie verdient aber wenig).
If we owned a castle (wir besitzen aber keines), we would have plenty of rooms for our guests and friends.
If I were / was you, I would stop smoking.

Merke:	***if*-Satz**	**Hauptsatz**
Typ I:	*simple present*	*will-future*
Typ II:	*past tense*	*conditional I*

Typ I: If I get your adress, I will write you a letter (= falls ich sie bekomme).
Typ II: If I got your adress, I would write you a letter (= ich bekomme sie wohl nicht).

Aufgepasst: Im *if*-Satz darf kein *will-future* oder *conditional* stehen!

ÜBUNG 1 **Bilde Sätze mit Satzteilen aus beiden Wortspeichern. Beginne jeden Satz mit *if* und schreibe in dein Übungsheft.**

you get some tickets
you're busy now
you don't hurry
you need money
you're hungry
you go by bus

we can have lunch now
we will go to the concert
we can talk later
it will be cheaper
we will be late again
I can lend you some

ÜBUNG 2 **Kreuze hinter jedem der folgenden Sätze an, um welchen Typ Bedingungssatz es sich handelt.**

	Typ I	Typ II
If I know the answer, I'll tell you.	☐	☐
If he loved jazz, you would like this CD.	☐	☐
Use my mobile phone if you need it.	☐	☐
Will you go to the party if they invite you?	☐	☐
If it were warmer, we could go for a walk.	☐	☐

ÜBUNG 3 **Bilde Bedingungssätze entweder des Typs I oder des Typs II.**

a good film / on TV tonight – the Johnsons / watch TV (Typ I)

you / think hard – you / get / a good idea (Typ I)

Joe's mum / give up work – more time / for her children (Typ II)

they all come / to her party – to be wonderful (Typ I)

not so much traffic – the air / cleaner (Typ II)

ÜBUNG 4 **Vervollständige die folgenden Sätze mit einem Bedingungssatz Typ II. Achtung: Aus verneinten Aussagen werden bejahte *if*-Sätze und umgekehrt!**

It rains. If it didn't rain ____, we could go by bike.

I have a lot to do today. If I ____ so much to do, we could go out.

I don't understand these questions. If I ____ them, I could help you with your homework.

The world isn't a better place. If the world ____ a better place, there would be no wars.

Sarah enjoys her work. She wouldn't do it if she ____.

ÜBUNG 5 **Setze das Verb in den Klammern in die passende Form.**

If Jane lived in the city, she ____ (not to be) happy.

If I ____ (to see) an accident, I would call the police at once.

What would you do if you ____ (not to have) a job?

Pat would fall asleep if she ____ (to get) bored.

If I were you, I ____ (to put on) a coat.

If Mr Baxter ____ (to win) a million pounds, he would go on a journey around the world.

Where would you go on holiday if your parents ____ (to ask) you to plan a trip for the summer?

WISSEN

Das Wort *würde*
Die Übersetzung des deutschen Wortes *würde* führt häufig zu Fehlern.

Merke: Nur im Hauptsatz wird *würde* mit *would* übersetzt!

Wenn ich nach London **ziehen würde,** …
→ If I **moved** to London, …
(nicht: If I ~~would move~~ to London, …)
Ich **würde** nach Hause **gehen,** wenn …
→ I **would go** home if …

ÜBUNG 6 **Übersetze die folgenden Sätze ins Englische und achte auf die richtige Übersetzung von *würde*. Schreibe in dein Übungsheft.**

Wenn ich mehr lesen würde, wäre ich besser informiert.
Wenn Sally Pete Geld leihen würde, würde er es ihr nicht zurückgeben.
Was würdest du deinem Brieffreund schreiben, wenn du von ihm einen Brief bekommen würdest?
Wir könnten zusammen Hausaufgaben machen, wenn wir uns treffen würden.

ÜBUNG 7 **Höre dir Track 6 auf der CD an und ergänze die folgenden Sätze.**

6

If Jan lived in England, __________.

Jan would be late for school __________.

He will cycle to school today __________.

If he waits, __________.

If the summer is warm and sunny, Jan and his friends __________.

But they must go by bus __________.

ÜBUNG 8 **Beantworte die Fragen mithilfe eines Bedingungssatzes. Schreibe die Sätze in dein Übungsheft.**

Beispiel: Shall we catch the 8:45 train? – No. (to arrive / too early)
→ If we took the 8:45 train, we would arrive too early.

Is Jack going to take the exam? – No. (to fail)
Will we stay at a hotel in London? – No. (to cost too much money)
Why don't we invite Robert to our party? – (to have to invite his friends, too)
Is Sally going to work in an office? – No. (to get bored)
Is Jeremy going to tell his teacher the truth? – No. (not to believe him)

ÜBUNG 9 **Benutze eigene Ideen, um die nachstehenden Sätze zu vervollständigen. Achtung: Bedingungssatz Typ I oder Typ II?**

If I study more for my exams, __________.

I would feel angry if __________.

If I didn't go to school tomorrow, __________.

Would you go to a party if __________?

If my parents allow me to, __________.

Would you mind if __________?

7.2 Notwendige und nicht notwendige Relativsätze

Es gibt im Englischen zwei Arten von **Relativsätzen:**

- den **notwendigen** Relativsatz *(defining relative clause)* und
- den **nicht notwendigen** Relativsatz *(non-defining relative clause).*

Die Relativsätze werden durch folgende **Relativpronomen** eingeleitet:

- ***which*** bezieht sich auf Dinge / Tiere,
- ***who / whom*** (sehr förmlich) bezieht sich auf Menschen,
- ***that*** bezieht sich auf Dinge, Tiere und Menschen und kann nur in *defining relative clauses* benutzt werden,
- ***whose*** entspricht dem deutschen ***dessen / deren*** und bezieht sich auf Dinge und Personen.

You always talk about things **which** I don't understand.
I'm crazy about a boy **who** likes football.
This is the man **who(m)** I told everything.
My friend likes girls **who / that** own a lot of money.
History is the subject **which / that** I like best.
Sarah knows a boy **whose** mum has a little shop.

Notwendige Relativsätze

Notwendige Relativsätze *(defining relative clauses)* sind für das Verständnis des Haupsatzes unentbehrlich, denn sie geben wichtige Informationen. Aus diesem Grund können sie **nicht weggelassen** werden.

Zwischen dem Hauptsatz und dem notwendigen Relativsatz steht **kein Komma.**

Notwendige Relativsätze werden durch die Relativpronomen ***which, who / whom, whose*** oder ***that*** eingeleitet.

The boy who / that is talking to Mr Miller is new here.
Don't forget the CD which / that I gave you last week.
My father was a man whom many people will never forget.
Those are the people whose house is next to ours.

Nicht notwendige Relativsätze

Nicht notwendige Relativsätze *(non-defining relative clauses)* sind Nebensätze, die zusätzliche Informationen enthalten und daher **nicht unbedingt** für das Gesamtverständnis des Satzes notwendig sind.

This actor, who lives in London now, is famous because of his last film.
We landed in Gatwick, which is London's second largest airport.
My father's car, whose door I left open, is one of the fastest cars ever.

Nicht notwendige Relativsätze werden immer durch **ein Komma** vom Hauptsatz abgetrennt.

That kann im nicht notwendigen Relativsatz **nicht** verwendet werden.

Relativsätze ohne Relativpronomen

In notwendigen Relativsätzen kann das Relativpronomen **weggelassen** werden, wenn das Relativpronomen **Objekt** des Satzes ist. Solche Relativsätze nennt man *contact clauses.*

This is the photo of **my friend who / that I met** on a bus to London. → This is the photo of **my friend I met** on a bus to London.
Is this t**he T-shirt which / that you bought** in London last year? → Is this **the T-shirt you bought** in London last year?

Präpositionen im notwendigen Relativsatz können stehen:

- **hinter dem Verb,** wenn das Relativpronomen *who(m), which* oder *that* verwendet wird,
  This is the house that / which I lived **in.**
- ebenfalls **hinter dem Verb** in *contact clauses,*
  This is the house I lived **in.**
- **vor dem Relativpronomen,** wenn das Relativpronomen *who(m), which* oder *whose* ist.
  This is the house **in** which I lived.

Aufgepasst: Vor ***that*** kann nie eine Präposition stehen!

ÜBUNG 10 **Setze das fehlende Relativpronomen ein. Achte darauf, ob es sich um eine Sache oder eine Person handelt! Entscheide auch, ob du das Relativpronomen *that* in den folgenden Beispielen wählen kannst.**

Jerry is going to the cinema with the girl ______ lives next door.

I know the girl ______ father was in the accident last night.

Where's the newspaper ______ was lying on the sofa?

That's the man ______ I told you about.

Do you like people ______ like to show off *(angeben)?*

My sister has got a job ______ she really enjoys.

Is that the family ______ dog always sleeps in our garden?

ÜBUNG 11 **Höre dir die folgenden Definitionen auf Track 7 der CD zweimal an und ergänze dann die Relativsätze. Achte auch auf das passende Relativpronomen.**

7

A book is a thing ______.

A doctor is a person ______.

London is a city ______.

A plane is something ______.

A prince is a person ______.

A cat is an animal ______.

Buckingham Palace is a building ______.

A racket is something ______.

An architect is somebody ______.

WISSEN

whose* und *who's

Verwechsle nicht ***whose*** und ***who's!***

- Bei *whose* handelt es sich um das besitzanzeigende Relativpronomen,
- *who's* ist die Kurzform von *who is.*

That's Mr Kent, whose (dessen) car has been in an accident.
Who's (wer ist) the boy over there?

ÜBEN

ÜBUNG 12 **Notwendiger oder nicht notwendiger Relativsatz? Entscheide, ob du bei den folgenden Sätzen ein Komma setzen musst oder nicht.**

I met a woman ___ who can speak six languages.

Jim always wears trousers ___ that are too big for him.

My father ___ who lived in York two years ago ___ loves nature.

Joanne K. Rowling ___ whose Harry Potter novels are world-famous ___ lives in Scotland.

The people ___ that work in that office ___ are very friendly.

My cousin lives in a house ___ which is 500 years old.

The man ___ who phoned this afternoon ___ didn't give his name.

Somebody has stolen my bike ___ I bought last year.

ÜBUNG 13 **Mache aus den zwei Sätzen einen Satz, indem du sie mit einem Relativpronomen verbindest. Welche Sätze sind *contact clauses?* Kennzeichne sie durch Einklammern des Relativpronomens.**

A woman was opening the door. She was wearing red jeans.

The woman ______________________________.

A policeman stopped my bike. He was very nice.

______________________________.

Sue is wearing an anorak. I like it.

______________________________.

Some pupils took their exams. They weren't difficult at all.

______________________________.

You bought some apples. How much were they?

______________________________.

You gave me a CD. I can't find it anywhere.

______________________________.

You made this cake. It was wonderful.

______________________________.

ÜBUNG 14 **Erkläre die folgenden Substantive mit einem Relativsatz und einer Präposition. Schreibe alle Möglichkeiten auf, mit denen der Relativsatz mit Präposition gebildet werden kann.**

1. key – to open a door with

   A key is something with ______________________.

   A key is something ______________________.

   A key is something ______________________.

2. chair – to sit on

   ______________________.

   ______________________.

   ______________________.

3. mirror – to look in

   ______________________.

   ______________________.

   ______________________.

ÜBUNG 15 **Verbessere die Sätze, indem du das falsche Relativpronomen durchstreichst und den Satz richtig in deinem Übungsheft aufschreibst.**

ACHTUNG FEHLER

Beispiel: That's the school ~~to that~~ I go. → That's the school that I go to.

Is that the girl who's photo was in the papers yesterday?

That's the hotel at whose we stayed.

Where is the lady which lost her purse?

Where is the pen with that I always write?

That's the boy who sister is good at French.

ÜBUNG 16 **Übersetze die deutschen Relativsätze ins Englische und schreibe die ganzen Sätze in dein Übungsheft.**

Is that the family deren Sohn gestern im Fernsehen war?
Where is the computer magazine das ich gerade gekauft habe?
That's the girl neben dem ich in der Schule sitze.
The house das meine Eltern gekauft haben has a garden and a pond.

7.3 Adverbialsätze

Adverbialsätze *(adverbial clauses)* sind durch einleitende **Konjunktionen** mit dem Hauptsatz verbunden.	Grandma often falls asleep **while** she is watching TV.
Ein Adverbialsatz kann **vor** oder **nach dem Hauptsatz** stehen. Steht er davor, dann wird gewöhnlich ein Komma benutzt.	**When** I entered the living room, Grandma was already sleeping.
Adverbialsätze der Zeit *(adverbial clauses of time)* (↑ Temporalsätze Kap. 7.5):	
when (wenn, als), as (als), as soon as (sobald), till / until (bis), before (bevor), since (seit, seitdem), while (während, solange)	I'll phone you **as soon as / when** I arrive in York. You're not going out **until** you have finished this.
Adverbialsätze des Ortes *(adverbial clauses of place):*	
where (wo), everywhere (überall), *wherever (wohin auch immer)*	Please leave the books **where** you found them. **Wherever / Everywhere** she goes, there are people waiting to see her.
Adverbialsätze des Grundes *(adverbial clauses of reason):*	
because (weil), as (da)	We are leaving **because** we are tired. **As** she grew older, she changed a lot.
Adverbialsätze der Einräumung / des Gegensatzes *(adverbial clauses of constrast):*	
while (während), even if (auch wenn), although / though (obwohl / obgleich)	**Although / Even if** it was already quite late, Sue was still working on her essay.
Adverbialsätze des Zwecks / der Folge *(adverbial clauses of purpose):*	
so / so that (sodass, damit)	I have so many CDs **so that** I don't know where to put them.
Adverbialsätze des Vergleichs *(adverbial sentences of comparison):*	
as (wie, so wie), as if / as though (als ob)	The cat is sitting in front of the radio **as if** it is listening to the programme.

ÜBUNG 17 **Verbinde die Satzteile zu sinnvollen Sätzen. Schreibe sie in dein Übungsheft.**

They went on	as soon as you can.
It was a difficult walk	because the holiday was over.
They were playing tennis	until they came to a small farm.
They turned back	so that they came home very tired.
Mr Campbell warned them about the dangers	before they left.
Get back	although it started to rain.
I felt really sorry	when the weather changed.

ÜBUNG 18 **Entscheide dich für die richtige Konjunktion und unterstreiche sie.**

The tour guide always warns the tourists before / because they leave.

We wanted to get back so that / as soon as we could.

Our neighbours went out because / although the weather was bad.

Give me your phone number so that / before I can phone you.

You should wait before / until the weather forecast is really good.

ÜBUNG 19 **Vervollständige die folgenden Sätze mithilfe einer passenden Konjunktion und den angegebenen Satzbausteinen.**

while – where – as if – wherever

she was sitting – the place – they are paying attention – I go

The beach is __________ I most like to be in the summer.

It is terribly loud __________ .

There was a huge bird above her __________ in the garden.

The students are sitting behind their desks __________ to their teacher.

ÜBEN

WISSEN

Adverbialsätze des Grundes
Because wird eher in nachgestellten Adverbialsätzen verwendet, mit *as* und *since* eingeleitete Adverbialsätze werden gewöhnlich vorangestellt.

As it is so cold today, I'll wear trousers.
Since Katie has no money, she can't afford the ticket.
I have to work hard because I'm going to take an exam soon.

ÜBUNG 20 **Höre dir Track 8 auf der CD zweimal an und beantworte die Fragen in deinem Übungsheft. Verwende bei der Beantwortung der Fragen die Konjunktionen aus dem Wortspeicher.**

8

although – until – because – if – then

Why is Kim a naughty girl?
What is a pity?
What did she do after she had watched a programme about animals in Africa?
How long did she play cards with her parents?
What will Kim do next weekend?

ÜBUNG 21 **Benutze jeweils eine der folgenden Konjunktionen und vervollständige die Sätze über deine letzten Ferien. Schreibe die Sätze in dein Übungsheft.**

as soon as – until – when – although – so that – because

I had a great time ...
I really enjoyed the holiday ...
I felt at home ...
I'd like to try a holiday in the USA next year ...
We had a lot of fun ...
It was a fantastic holiday ...

7.4 Objektergänzungen

Notwendige Objektergänzung

Bei bestimmten Verben steht **nach dem direkten Objekt** noch eine notwendige Ergänzung zu diesem Objekt *(object complement)*.

Diese Ergänzung kann ein **Substantiv** oder ein **Adjektiv** sein.

They call this place Piano Bar. (→ die Ergänzung “Piano Bar” ist ein Substantiv)
He found life very hard. (→ die Ergänzung “hard” ist ein Adjektiv)

Nach folgenden Verben steht nach dem direkten Objekt eine notwendige Ergänzung:

to call – nennen	My name is George. But my wife calls me Georgie.
to crown – krönen zu	When was Henry VIII crowned king?
to declare – erklären zu	This area was declared a national park in 1998.
to find – finden, halten für	We didn’t find the film boring.
to make – machen	The test results made our English teacher very angry.
to think – halten für	My parents think sports useful.

Daraus ergibt sich folgende Satzstellung:
Subjekt + Verb + Objekt + Ergänzung

Objektergänzung mit *as*

Aufgepasst: Bei manchen Verben wird die Objektergänzung mit der Präposition ***as*** angeschlossen:

to choose as – wählen zu	The company chose Mrs Smith as a chairwoman.
to describe as – beschreiben als	My mum often describes me as a very lazy boy.
to treat as – behandeln wie	Some teachers treat us as criminals.

ÜBUNG 22 **Wie kannst du etwas nennen? Benutze die Adjektive aus dem vorangegangenen Satz und verwende *to call*.**

The hotel is wonderful. – Really? I don't ______.

What a lovely meal! – How can you ______?

This man is miserable. – Oh no! You can't ______.

ÜBUNG 23 **Wähle jeweils ein Adjektiv oder ein Substantiv aus dem Wortspeicher und ergänze damit die folgenden Sätze.**

necessary – difficult – an idiot – nervous – king – as a close friend

This exam makes me ______.

Who crowned him ______?

The class found these exercises ______.

Stop calling me ______.

All my teachers think homework ______.

Can you describe Marc ______?

ÜBUNG 24 **Kennst du dich in Großbritannien aus? Ergänze die Sätze mit deinen eigenen Ideen.**

People in Great Britain are friendly. They make you feel ______.

You should visit the capital of Great Britain. I'm sure you'll find it ______.

Have you ever been to Wales? You call the people there ______.

People in Scotland wear skirts. You call those skirts ______.

You should visit London and its sights. You'll find them ______.

Have you ever tried baked beans? Some people think them ______.

Those buses in London are world-famous. People call them ______.

I hope you have good weather. Good weather always makes a holiday ______.

7.5 Temporalsätze

Temporalsätze oder Adverbialsätze der Zeit *(clauses of time)* geben an, **wann** etwas geschieht.	
Temporalsätze werden mit verschiedenen **Konjunktionen** eingeleitet. Zu ihnen gehören:	
as soon as – sobald	Kim will phone her parents as soon as she arrives in New York.
as – als, während	She was watching him as he was getting ready.
till / until – bis	You are not going out until you have finished this.
before – bevor	Lock the doors before you leave.
when – als, wenn	When we arrived, we were welcomed by the whole family.
since – seit	What have you been doing since we last met?
while – während	While I was waiting at the bus stop, it started to rain.
Aufgepasst: ***If*** und ***when*** können beide mit *wenn* übersetzt werden, haben aber dennoch unterschiedliche Bedeutung:	
■ *If* leitet einen Bedingungssatz (= falls) ein,	If I'm late this evening, don't wait for me.
■ *when* (= sobald) einen Temporalsatz.	When I get home this evening, I'm going to have a shower.
Der Unterschied zwischen ***as*** und ***when:***	
■ *As* wird benutzt, wenn zwei Dinge zur gleichen Zeit passieren,	As I walked into the room, the phone started ringing.
■ *when* wird benutzt, wenn eins nach dem anderen passiert.	When I got home, I had a bath.
In Temporalsätzen wird auch dann, wenn über ein zukünftiges Ereignis gesprochen wird, nicht die Zukunftsform des Verbs benutzt. Die **Zukunft** wird nur im **Hauptsatz** verwendet, während im **Nebensatz** das ***present tense*** steht.	We will stay here until you get back. The children won't be at home when we arrive.

ÜBUNG 25 Verbinde die Satzteile mit Linien zu sinnvollen Sätzen, indem du eine passende Konjunktion wählst.

I'll go to the United States	since	you come back.
Carol phoned a friend	as soon as	you go outside.
It began to rain	before	I'm 18.
Don't forget your coat	until	the teacher entered the room.
John will stay here	when	she came home.
The pupils have been quiet	while	Mr Lennox was working in the garden.

ÜBUNG 26 *If* oder *when?* – Entscheide dich für die richtige Konjunktion.

_______ I'm late tonight, don't wait for me.

I'm going to town. _______ I come back, we can have our tea.

Do you mind _______ I smoke in here?

David is still at school. _______ he leaves school, he wants to study.

_______ Tony uses his bike, he always wears his helmet.

ÜBUNG 27 Hier musst du dich zwischen *as* und *when* entscheiden. Verbinde die Satzteile mit Linien und wähle die richtige Konjunktion.

We were all waving goodbye	as	I was cycling along the street.
Sue smiled	when	I was preparing the vegetables.
I cut myself	as	Hugh drove away in his car.
A dog ran out in front of my bike	when	her father took a photo of her.

ÜBEN

ÜBUNG 28 **Bilde aus zwei Sätzen einen: Verbinde die beiden Hauptsätze zu einem Hauptsatz mit Temporalsatz + Konjunktion.**

We'll arrive back home tomorrow. Then I'll phone Sarah.

When we arrive back home tomorrow, I will phone Sarah.

Pat was drawing some pictures. There was some noise outside.

George must wait at home. Then his mum comes back.

First Marvin should eat something. Then he can go out with Kevin.

Mrs Jenkins sat down. At the same time the phone rang.

The pupils are standing at the bus stop. The bus hasn't arrived yet.

Jenny lives in Howard Road. She moved there last year.

ÜBUNG 29 **Vervollständige die Sätze mithilfe der Verben im Wortspeicher. Benutze die richtige Konjunktion und achte auf die richtige Zeit.**

to finish your homework – ~~to cross the road~~ – to come back –
to have a shower – to be away on holiday

Timmy, you must always look both ways before you cross the road.

Our neighbour will feed our cats ______.

I'm going to bed ______.

The Watsons will visit us ______.

I'll wait for you ______.

ÜBEN

Klassenarbeit 1

60 Minuten

AUFGABE 1 **Bilde vollständige *if*-Sätze, indem du die passenden Satzteile mit Linien verbindest. Achtung: Typ I oder Typ II?**

If you leave now	if we go to America next year.
If I knew the date	if she won the competition.
We'll visit my aunt in Washington	she'll be angry with herself.
If the book wasn't so expensive	you won't miss the bus.
Janet would be very happy	Sue would buy it.
If Mary does badly in her test next week	I would send Joe a birthday card.

AUFGABE 2 **Erkläre die Gegenstände auf den Bildern mithilfe eines Relativsatzes. Verwende die Satzteile und füge sie mit dem richtigen Relativpronomen zusammen.**

you can wear when it is cold outside – has got long ears – you can write a friend when you are on holiday – is a person – is something – an animal – takes you from one country to another one – a short letter – looks after sick animals – is something

A rabbit is ______________________________.

______________________________. 

______________________________.

______________________________. 

______________________________.

AUFGABE 3 **Entscheide dich für das richtige Relativpronomen und setze Kommas, falls nötig. Streiche bei *contact clauses* den Kasten durch.**

My neighbours have got a new cat ______ name is Sam.

Have you found your door key ______ you lost yesterday?

The English book ______ I'm reading is very difficult.

Elizabeth II ______ son is Prince Charles became Queen of England in 1952.

What is the English word for someone ______ doesn't eat meat?

Maggie works for a company ______ makes washing-machines.

Barbara ______ speaks French and Italian works as a tour guide.

I borrowed a book from the library ______ cover was already dirty.

AUFGABE 4 **Bilde Adverbialsätze mit den folgenden Satzteilen. Benutze die passenden Konjunktionen und achte auf die richtige Zeit.**

Yesterday / Jill / to slip / to get off the bus

The Robinsons / to have / their pond / they moved house

Mr Smith / to hate / loud music / it / to give him / a headache

Last night / Tom and Kate / to go / cinema / they / to be tired

We / must leave / for the show in good time / we / to get / good seats

You / to ruin / your eyes / you / read / in this bad light

My father / often / to eat / sweets / to work / on his computer

TESTEN

AUFGABE 5 **In den folgenden Sätzen sind Fehler versteckt. Erkenne sie und verbessere sie, indem du den ganzen Satz neu schreibst.**

ACHTUNG FEHLER

If you won't know the answer, you can ask me.

That's the boy who sister is going to London for a term.

If you arrive in York, I'll pick you up from the station.

If you wait a minute, I go with you.

Colin told me about his new job that he's enjoying very much.

Somebody stole my camera as I was on holiday.

If you would go by train, it would be quicker than by bus.

All the people which were at my party were friends of mine.

AUFGABE 6 **Übersetze die folgenden Adverbialsätze ins Englische und schreibe sie in dein Übungsheft.**

Wenn du rennst, dann wirst du den Bus noch bekommen.
Obwohl Janet sehr müde war, konnte sie nicht schlafen.
Sobald Herr Miller nach Hause kommt, schaltet er das Radio an.
Jack verließ die Party früher, weil er Kopfschmerzen hatte.
Wo wirst du übernachten, wenn du in London bist?
Während Jill am Strand war, las sie viel.

Klassenarbeit 2

45 Minuten

AUFGABE 7 **Bilde vollständige Sätze, indem du die passenden Satzteile mit Linien verbindest. Achte darauf, dass du die richtige Konjunktion wählst.**

We didn't get wet	wherever	the actors played their parts badly.
My dog is sitting behind the door	as if	the princess kissed it.
The film was terrible	when	we had fastened our seat belts.
It was foggy	as soon as	my father drove into London.
My friend always stops	although	to be waiting for me.
The plane took off	because	she sees a shoe shop.
My father bought a paper	after	it was raining.
The frog turned into a prince	so that	he could read the latest news.

AUFGABE 8 **Ergänze den zweiten Teil des Objekts mit den Ausdrücken aus dem Wortspeicher.**

very welcome – Sue – lochs – crazy – strange – pleasant

There are lot of lakes in Scotland. There you call them ________.

Sunshine and high temperatures always makes a holiday ________.

People in Ireland are friendly. They will always make you ________.

Have you heard about Sarah's plans? – Yes, but I find her idea ________.

Most people in our town find our neighbour a bit ________.

Her name is Susan. But I'm sure you can call her ________.

TESTEN

AUFGABE 9 **Aus zwei mach eins: Schreibe die folgenden Sätze um, indem du sie in Relativsätze verwandelst. Schreibe in dein Übungsheft. Unterstreiche dann die Relativpronomen, die einen *contact clause* einleiten.**

My parents met a man. He is my teacher.
The tourists visited a house. Sherlock Holmes lived there.
Mr Smith works in a factory. It produces mobiles.
The police questioned a woman. Her daughter had stolen some CDs.
I saw that film. You watched it the day before yesterday.
That body lotion has a terrible smell. My friend uses it.
Sue met a scientist. He won the Nobel Prize last year.
The old lady saw that man again. His house was burgled twice last year.

AUFGABE 10 **Vervollständige die folgenden Sätze mit der Verben in Klammer und weiteren passenden Ergänzungen. Achte darauf, dass der *if-clause* nicht immer am Anfang steht. Schreibe in dein Übungsheft.**

If I go on holiday, ... (to visit)
If the Queen invited me, ... (to have)
We'll be happy if we ... (to meet)
If I were rich, ... (to buy)
Brian will dance with Sally, if ... (to ask)
Open the window if ... (to be too warm)
We could go to the cinema tonight if Maggie ... (to come)
If Chris and his friends went to Rome, they ... (to see)

AUFGABE 11 **Übersetze die folgenden Sätze und achte auf die richtige Übersetzung der Objektergänzungen. Schreibe in dein Übungsheft.**

Schotten sollten nicht Engländer genannt werden.
Wann wurde Elizabeth I. zur Königin gekrönt?
Viele Eltern halten Obst und Gemüse für gesund.
Ich würde ihn als einen netten Jungen beschreiben.
Die Schüler finden das Buch spannend.
Behandele mich nicht wie ein Kind!

Die indirekte Rede

8.1 Die Veränderung der Pronomen

Mit der indirekten Rede *(reported speech)* gibt man wieder, was jemand sagt oder gesagt hat. Zur Einleitung der indirekten Rede verwendet man Verben des Sagens *(reporting verbs)* und einen *that*-Satz. Zu den Verben des Sagens gehören: *to say, to tell, to answer, to agree, to explain, to think*	Mike: "I'm coming back on Friday." → Mike **says that** he is coming back on Friday. George: "I like chocolate biscuits." → George **explains that** he likes chocolate biscuits.
Vor dem *that*-Satz steht kein Komma. *That* kann auch weggelassen werden.	She says she is tired.
Wenn sofort wiedergegeben wird, was jemand gesagt hat, so benutzt man für den Einleitungssatz das ***present tense***.	Andrew says: "I hate maths lessons." *present tense:* Andrew **says** (that) he hates maths lessons.
Wird etwas erst später wiedergegeben, so benutzt man einen Einleitungssatz im ***past tense.***	*past tense:* Andrew **said** (that) he hated maths lessons.
Steht das einleitende Verb im *past tense,* dann werden die Zeitformen der indirekten Rede zurückverschoben *(backshift of tenses)* (↑ Kap. 8.2).	
Wie im Deutschen zeigt die indirekte Rede auch im Englischen den Standpunkt der Person, die berichtet. Die **Pronomen** werden dem Standpunkt des Berichtenden angepasst.	
Personalpronomen: *I, you → he / she* *we, you → they*	Andy: "**I** can't help you with **your** homework, Jim." → Andy explains to Jim (that) **he** can't help **him** with **his** homework.
Possessivpronomen: *my, your → his / her* *me, you → him / her* *our, your → their* *us, you → them*	Linda: "**My** brother is usually nice to **me.**" → Linda tells me (that) **her** brother is usually nice to **her.**

WISSEN

ÜBUNG 1 **Berichte, was die folgenden Leute sagen.**

The girl says that ______________________________.

The girl told Linda that ______________________________.

My parents explain to me that ______________________________.

The kids think that ______________________________

______________________________.

ÜBUNG 2 **Höre die auf Track 9 der CD zweimal die Nachrichten an, die zwei Anrufer auf Mr Robertsons Anrufbeantworter hinterlassen haben. Mr Robertson teilt die Nachrichten seinem Sohn Bruce mit. Setze die fehlenden Pronomen in den Lückentext.**

9

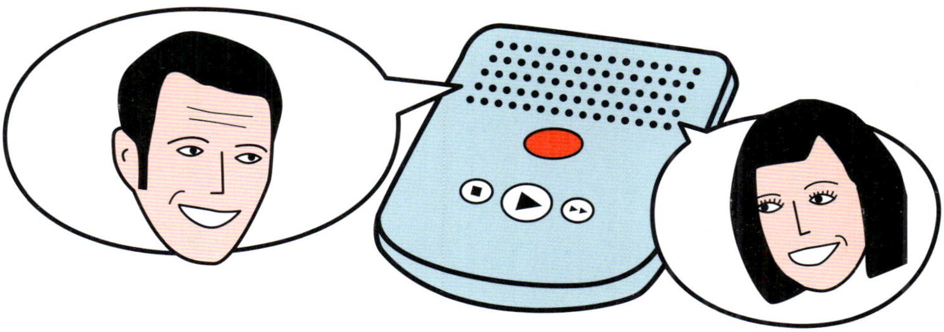

"Bruce, Mr Jefferson called. ________ can't give ________ ________ piano lesson next Tuesday. If ________ want a lesson on Wednesday, ________ should call ________ back before Tuesday. And Cindy called, too. There is something important that ________ has to tell ________ . ________ wants ________ to call ________ as soon as ________ get home."

ÜBUNG 3 **Wandle die Sätze in der indirekten Rede in die direkte Rede um.**

Lynn tells Richard that she is going to work in London.

Lynn to Richard: "_______________."

Sarah says she has forgotten to do her homework.

Sarah: "_______________."

Mr Hall thinks that his children shouldn't go to parties.

Mr Hall: "_______________."

His mother told Tim that he can't have a new computer.

His mother: "_______________."

WISSEN

***Say* oder *tell*?**

Auf ***say*** kann ein indirektes Objekt (Personenobjekt) folgen. Es muss dann **mit *to*** angeschlossen werden.

She **said (to me)** that she would be back late.
They **say (to us)** that we must hurry up.

Auf ***tell*** muss ein indirektes Objekt (Personenobjekt) folgen. Es wird **ohne *to*** angeschlossen.

She **told me** that she would be back late.
They **tell us** that we must hurry up.

ÜBUNG 4 ***Say* oder *tell* – setze in die Lücke das richtige Verb. Aufgepasst: Es ist nicht immer nur das *present tense* gefragt!**

Sue _______________ to her dad that she usually goes to bed early.

Andrew _______________ that he had had a wonderful holiday two years ago.

What did they _______________ you?

Did he _______________ his parents what had happened?

Vanessa never _______________ her mum anything about school.

They didn't _______________ a word to us. Have they _______________ you anything?

ÜBEN

8.2 Die Rückverschiebung der Zeiten

Steht das Verb des einleitenden Satzes im ***past tense*** (oder im ***past perfect***), dann werden die Zeiten in der indirekten Rede um eine Zeitstufe gegenüber der direkten Rede ***zurück in die Vergangenheit*** verschoben *(backshift of tenses).*

He said that ...
She had told me ...

Regeln zur *backshift of tenses*

Das Verschieben der Zeitformen erfolgt nach folgenden Regeln:

- *present tense → past tense*

  Pete: "I **write** my penfriend every week."
  → Pete said that he **wrote** his penfriend every week.

- *present progressive → past progressive*

  Sue: "We **are having** a really good time."
  → Sue told me that they **were having** a really good time.

- *present perfect → past perfect*

  Tim: "I **have lost** my keys somewhere."
  → Tim said he **had lost** his keys somewhere.

- *past tense → past perfect*

  Mary: "I **saw** Janet in the park."
  → Mary told me that she **had seen** Janet in the park.

- *going-to-future → was / were going to*

  Pete: "I **am going to** fly to China."
  → Pete said he **was going to** fly to China.

- *will-future → would + infinitive*

  Tom: "I **will pass** the exam."
  → Tom told me that he **would pass** the exam.

- *can → could*

  Claire: "I **can** understand my parents."
  → Claire said she **could** understand her parents.

- *may → might*

  Ann: "I **may** go to the cinema."
  → Ann said she **might** go to the cinema.

ÜBUNG 5 **Wandle die Sätze, die gesagt werden, in die indirekte Rede um. Achte auf das Verb im Einleitungssatz!**

Fiona: "I don't want to do anything."

Fiona said ______________________________.

Beth: "My friend and I will probably visit some friends in Scotland."

Beth told me that ______________________________.

Brian: "I have already spent my pocket money on comics."

Brian told us that ______________________________.

Lucy: "I work at the supermarket every Saturday."

Lucy said ______________________________.

Dave: "I may not be at home on Sunday."

Dave said ______________________________.

Sophie: "I was ill on Wednesday."

Sophie told me that ______________________________.

ÜBUNG 6 **Gestern hast du dich mit Judy unterhalten. Heute erzählst du deiner besten Freundin / deinem besten Freund, worüber ihr gesprochen habt. Schreibe in dein Übungsheft.**

Judy said her parents …
Then I told her …

ÜBUNG 7 **Sage auf die folgenden Aussagen immer das Gegenteil, indem du die Sätze jeweils mit *I thought you said* einleitest.**

This snack bar is expensive. → Is it? I thought you said it was cheap.

Ann isn't coming to the party on Saturday. → Really? ______

______.

Helen likes Paul. → Does she? ______

______.

I'll be in London on Monday. → Will you? ______

______ in Manchester.

I can speak a little French. → Can you? ______

______.

I haven't been to the cinema for ages. → Haven't you? ______

______ last Sunday.

WISSEN

Keine Rückverschiebung der Zeiten

Die *backshift of tenses* **unterbleibt,** wenn

- das Verb der direkten Rede im ***past perfect*** oder im ***conditional*** *(might / could / would)* steht,

  Tom: "I **hadn't tidied** my room when my parents came home." → Tom told me that he **hadn't tidied** his room when his parents had come home.
  Sue: "I **might watch** the film on TV." → Sue said she **might watch** the film on TV.

- in der direkten Rede ***must / needn't*** steht. Allerdings kann *must* auch durch *had to* und *needn't* durch *didn't have to* ersetzt werden.

  Dennis: "I **must** fly home on the 6th." → Dennis said he **must** (auch: **had to**) fly home on the 6th.

Wenn in der direkten Rede eine allgemein gültige Aussage steht oder zum Zeitpunkt der Wiedergabe noch zutrifft, kann die Rückverschiebung entfallen (sie wäre aber nicht falsch).

Andy: "My sister **studies** at the University of London." → Andy told us that his sister **studies** (*auch:* **studied**) at the University of London.

ÜBUNG 8 **Setze die Sätze in die indirekte Rede. Achtung: *backshift* oder nicht?**

Dave: "I hadn't expected to get a job."

Dave told me that ______________________________.

Sally: "I would like to be an actor some day."

Sally said that ______________________________.

Nora: "It might be difficult to get a job."

Nora told her friends ______________________________.

My parents: "You must be back at 11 o'clock!"

My parents told me that ______________________________.

Peter to his penfriend: "School in Germany starts at 8 o'clock."

Peter wrote his penfriend ______________________________.

ÜBUNG 9 **Setze die Verben in den Klammern in die richtige Zeit. Achte darauf, dass es sich bei den Sätzen um die indirekte Rede handelt!**

Some pupils were talking about homework. One boy said he ______________ (to do) homework for three hours every evening. Some pupils also said that they ______________ (not – to do) their homework yet.

Vicky told her teacher that she ______________ (to feel) ill.

Leo said that he ______________ (to phone) his mother from York.

Mrs Hall told me that Tom and Jill ______________ (to be) at their aunt's.

Lynn told Jim that he ______________ (may see) her at Becky's party.

WISSEN

Adverbialbestimmungen
Adverbialbestimmungen ändern sich nur, wenn das einleitende Verb in der Vergangenheit steht:

here → there, two weeks ago → two weeks before, this / these → that / those, tomorrow → the next day, next week → the following week, today → that day

Karen: "It's my birthday **today.** I'm going to celebrate **here.**" → Karen told me that it was her birthday **that day.** She said she was going to celebrate **there.**

ÜBUNG 10 **Gib die folgenden Sätze in der indirekten Rede wieder. Achte dabei auf die Zeit des einleitenden Verbs!**

Tim: "I haven't saved enough money for the concert ticket."

Tim told me that ______________________.

Sarah: "Robin's party is at 7:30."

Sarah says ______________________.

Doctor: "You must eat more fruit and vegetables."

The doctor tells Mrs Hall that ______________________.

Sally: "I will meet my exchange partner at the station."

Sally explained to her parents that ______________________

______________________.

Anna: "John is going to buy a new computer."

Anna said ______________________.

Aunt Molly: "Judy can stay for the time being."

Aunt Molly tells my mum that ______________________.

ÜBUNG 11 **Streiche die Fehler in den folgenden Sätzen an. Schreibe dann jeweils den ganzen verbesserten Satz in dein Übungsheft.**

ACHTUNG FEHLER

My cousin said he will meet me in front of the restaurant.

Richard told James that he is going to buy a new computer.

Mr Dixon said he hasn't been to the cinema since 2001.

George told me that he can help with my English homework.

Tina said me that her parents had been strict when she was young.

ÜBUNG 12 **Übersetze die folgenden Sätze und schreibe sie in dein Übungsheft.**

Jane sagt, dass Mary gut in Biologie sei.
Mary sagte mir, dass sie später kommen werde.
Ann und Michael sagten, dass sie am Wochenende ins Kino gehen wollten.
Jenny sagt ihrer Mutter, dass sie einen Freund eingeladen hat.
Tom sagte, dass er 2008 angefangen habe, Gitarre zu spielen.

Klassenarbeit 1

45 Minuten

AUFGABE 1 **Liz nimmt ein Telefonat für ihren Bruder Robbie entgegen, der gerade duscht. Liz berichtet ihrem Bruder, was Emma am Telefon sagt. Achte auf die Pronomen in der indirekten Rede!**

Emma: "I can't pick him up at seven. My mother's car has broken down."

Liz: "Robbie, Emma says she ____________________

____________________."

Emma: "Perhaps I can have my father's car."

Liz: "She says perhaps she ____________________

____________________."

Emma: "If not, we will have to go to the theatre by underground."

Liz: "She says if not, ____________________

____________________."

Emma: "My mum has already bought the tickets for us."

Liz: "____________________."

AUFGABE 2 **Setze die folgenden Sätze in die indirekte Rede. Achte auf das einleitende Verb!**

George: "My sister has had a new car for two weeks."

George said ____________________.

Sarah: "I don't like fish."

Sarah has just told me ____________________.

Mr Dexter: "I have never spoken to Jane's teacher."

Mr Dexter explained to his wife that ____________________.

The policeman: "Some drivers can be really careless."

The policeman explains to us that ____________________.

Sue: "After I had come home from school, I had something to eat."

Sue said that ____________________.

TESTEN

AUFGABE 3 **Entscheide dich für das richtige Verb: *to say* oder *to tell*.**

Sonia ______ me that you were ill.

What did you ______ the police?

Anne ______ goodbye to me and left.

______ us about your holiday. Did you have a nice time?

Don't just stand there! ______ something!

I wonder where Sue is. She ______ she would be here at 8 o'clock.

Ralph couldn't help me. He ______ me to ask Kate.

AUFGABE 4 **Verwandle die folgenden Sätze zurück in die direkte Rede.**

John told me that he was very happy.

John: "______."

Peter said that he didn't know where Janet was.

Peter: "______."

Sarah said that she was ill a few days ago.

Sarah: "______."

The pupils told their teacher that their bus had been late again.

The pupils: "______."

Jack said that he hoped he would be able to come.

Jack: "______."

AUFGABE 5 **Übersetze die folgenden Sätze ins Englische. Schreibe sie in dein Übungsheft.**

Jeff sagte mir, dass Sue krank sei.
Anne und Michael sagten, dass sie Tennis spielen wollen.
Tom sagte mir, dass er keinen Tee mag.
Mrs Brown sagt, dass sie jeden Tag früh aufstehe.
Julias Eltern sagten ihr, dass sie dieses Kleid nicht in der Schule tragen könne.

Klassenarbeit 2

30 Minuten

AUFGABE 6 **Setze die Verben in Klammer in die richtige Zeitform. Achte immer auf das einleitende Verb.**

She told us that she _____ (not to like) the new film.

Mum asked me what I _____ (to do) all morning.

The pupils told their teacher that they _____ (just / to finish) the exercise.

My friend said that he _____ (not to see) me the next day.

Stephanie told her friend that she _____ (to be ill) on Friday.

AUFGABE 7 **Schreibe die folgenden Sätze von der indirekten Rede in die direkte Rede um. Schreibe in dein Übungsheft.**

Anne says that her birthday party starts at 7:30.
They told us that Tracy had to do the exam again because she had cheated.
The policeman wanted us to lock our doors at night.
Mrs Braddock said that her son wasn't going to school that day because he was sick.
My mum wanted to know if I had already tidied my room
Tom tells me that his parents were angry because he didn't do the washing up the day before.

AUFGABE 8 **Schreibe folgende Aussagen in der indirekten Rede in dein Übungsheft.**

"She was the most beautiful girl in my school." → Jane told me ...
"I'm having a party tomorrow. Are you coming?" → Frances says / asks ...
"I'm sure Robert will help you. He often helps people." → My friend mentioned ...
"Don't forget to water the flowers!" → My parents tell me ...
"Can you give me your homework on Monday?" → Joe wanted to know ...
"I had a terrible accident yesterday. I broke my foot." → She said ...
"When did you last meet Mr Sly?" → Mr Brown asked ...
"You can pass the exam." → My teacher keeps on telling me ...

9 Englisch lernen

9.1 Thematischer Lernwortschatz

Der Wortschatz im Englischen lässt sich in einen Grundwortschatz und einen Aufbauwortschatz aufteilen.

Der **Grundwortschatz** beinhaltet die häufigsten Wörter, Wortverbindungen und Redewendungen. Mit ihm kannst du Gespräche auf Englisch führen oder auch schon Briefe an einen englischen oder amerikanischen Brieffreund schreiben.

transport and travelling: bus, plane, underground, ferry, to go by, to walk, to fly, to land, to drive, to sail

Der **Aufbauwortschatz** baut auf den Grundwortschatz auf und erweitert diesen. Er hilft dir, dich zu einem bestimmten Sachverhalt mit einem breit gefächerten Vokabular zu äußern.

transport and travelling: coach (Reisebus), underground network (U-Bahnnetz), destination (Reiseziel), dining car (Speisewagen), sleepers (Schlafwagen), to depart (abfahren), on schedule (pünktlich)

Im Unterricht lernst du Vokabeln meist in einem inhaltlichen Zusammenhang: Jede Lektion ist einem **Themenschwerpunkt** zugeordnet. Daher ist es sinnvoll, Vokabeln auch nach Themen zu lernen. Hilfreich sind **Wortfelder, Bilder** oder **Diagramme *(mind maps).***

Themenschwerpunkt "school": primary school (Grundschule), secondary school (weiterführende Schule), comprehensive school (Gesamtschule), boarding school (Internat), school report (Zeugnis)

Weitere **Tipps zum Vokabellernen:**

- Lerne in **kleinen Lernportionen:** höchstens 30 Vokabeln pro Tag, am besten in drei Zehnerblöcke aufgeteilt.
- Lege eine **Lernkartei** an: Sortiere Wörter, die du zweimal gewusst hast, aus und konzentriere dich auf die Vokabeln, die du nicht beherrschst.
- Schreibe besonders schwierige Vokabeln auf gut sichtbar aufgehängte **Lernplakate** oder **-poster.**
- Sprich (nicht mehr als zehn) Vokabeln auf einen Kassettenrekorder oder ein **Diktiergerät:** mit Pausen zum Nachsprechen oder Übersetzen.

Wortfeld "temperature": hot, warm, cool, cold; *"travelling":* ticket, passport, suitcase

Diagramm *(mind map)* "clothes":

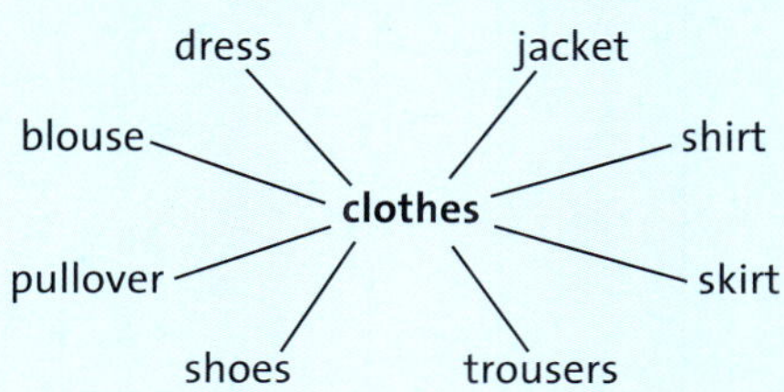

ÜBUNG 1 **In der Stadt – was ist auf den folgenden Bildern dargestellt?**

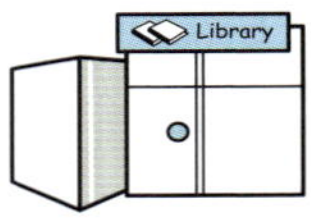

______

______

______

______

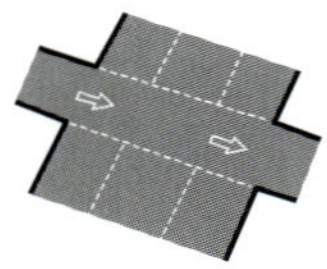

______

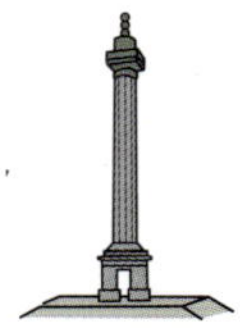

______

ÜBUNG 2 **Finde das Gegenteil zu den folgenden Begriffen.**

town ↔ ______

quiet ↔ ______

mountain ↔ ______

boring ↔ ______

in the city ↔ ______

stressful ↔ ______

ÜBUNG 3 **Vervollständige den folgenden Text mit den richtigen Ausdrücken.**

This city is fantastic. There are theatres and cinemas, so there's ______ to see. Let's ______ a bus to go to the museum. Every year many tourists go ______ in London. If we want to go shopping, we must go ______. Some people don't live in the centre of a city but in the ______.

A lot of farmers use their fields to ______ potatoes and vegetables.

If you spend your holidays on a farm you can enjoy the ______ ______. We could go for a walk in the nearby ______ – there are lovely trees.

A nature reserve is an ______ of land where the animals and plants are protected.

ÜBUNG 4 Verbinde die Adjektive mit den passenden Substantiven.

rich	factory
flat	farmland
large	museum
wild	area
ugly	forest
hilly	landscape
fascinating	city
crowded	rock

ÜBUNG 5 Benutze nun die Ausdrücke aus der Übung 4 und schreibe die Dinge auf, die du positiv und negativ am Stadtleben oder Landleben findest. Formuliere sechs Sätze und begründe deine Antworten. Die Ausdrücke im Wortspeicher können dir dabei behilflich sein.

I like / don't like ... – I hate ... – I can't stand ... –
I think ... is / are OK – I think ... is good / terrible / ...

ÜBUNG 6 Beschreibe in vier bis sechs Sätzen die Gegend, in der du wohnst. Benutze weitgehend Vokabeln aus diesem Kapitel.

9.2 Text- und Hörverständnis

Lesen und Verstehen

Zunächst fragt man nach der **Textsorte:** Handelt es sich um eine Geschichte, einen Bericht, einen Brief, ein Theaterstück, ein Gedicht oder eine Informationsbroschüre?

What kind of text is it? → The text is a story / report / letter / play / poem ...

Der nächste Schritt ist die Frage nach dem **Thema des Textes.** Dabei kann die Überschrift, der Einleitungssatz oder das Bildmaterial von großer Hilfe sein.

What is the text about? → The story / report is about ..., It has / gives important facts / information about ...

When you read the headline / first passage you expect to read about ...

Beim Lesen sollte man den Text sowohl in seiner Gesamtheit als auch seine Details erfassen können.

- Zum **Gesamtverständnis** helfen Überschrift, Schlüsselwörter *(key-words),* Bilder oder der erste Textabschnitt.

The Romans in Europe; The Roman Empire

- Zum **Detailverständnis** liest man den Text ein zweites Mal und macht sich zu den Schlüsselwörtern **Notizen.**

"Roman baths":
- daily life
- important role for the hygiene
- social function

- **Unbekannte Wörter** können aus dem Textzusammenhang erschlossen werden.

The Roman baths had "changing rooms". → A changing room has got something to do with "to change" and the context is about a bath. → „Umkleidekabine"

Hörverstehen

Lies dir zunächst die Fragestellung gründlich durch, damit du weißt, worauf du beim Hören achten musst.
Mache dir während der Hördurchgänge Notizen. Die zuvor gelesenen Aufgabenstellungen helfen dir dabei.
Beantworte danach die Fragen, kreuze die richtigen Antworten an oder verbessere falsche Aussagen.
Höre dir notfalls die CD ein weiteres Mal an.

ÜBUNG 7 **Versuche anhand des Bildes und der Überschrift herauszufinden, wovon ein darauf folgender Text handeln könnte. Begründe deine Antwort.**

Sarah's first holiday alone

ÜBUNG 8 **Lies nun den dazugehörigen Text aufmerksam durch.**

When the train arrived, it was almost empty. Sarah Hill had already been standing on platform 9 at King's Cross Station in London for about ten minutes. It was a sunny day, almost cloudless. Sarah had just said good-bye to her father. She was on her way to Yorkshire to visit her mother who worked there as a vet.

Sarah lived with her father in London, the city of cities. She loved London, so she had decided to stay here with her father instead of moving up North when her parents had separated.

Sarah's father didn't like the wild countryside. He always said life in a big city was the only true life. That was one reason for her parents' separation: Mum didn't like big cities because they are dirty, smelly and noisy. She was fond of animals, and she loved her job.

And now Sarah would spend two weeks in Yorkshire. Her mum would meet her in York. She had already told Sarah on the phone about the beautiful landscape, sheep farms, endless fields and the soft green hills.

Sarah got on the train. She was excited: It was her first visit after her parents had split up two years ago, and it was her first holiday without her father. Mr Hill had bought the train tickets, had given her some pocket money and had helped her with the bags. Her father was great – simply helpful and understanding; sometimes strict but never really angry with Sarah.

The train started, and while Sarah, who had her own compartment, was paging through "Mizz Seventeen", her favourite teen mag, the suburbs of London passed by. What if she liked Yorkshire and didn't want to come back ...?

ÜBUNG 9 **Um welche Textsorte handelt es sich bei dem vorliegenden Text? Was erwartest du weiterhin von einem solchen Text? Formuliere zwei Sätze.**

ÜBUNG 10 **Unterstreiche die unbekannten Wörter im Text, schreibe sie heraus und versuche sie aus dem Zusammenhang zu erklären.**

ÜBUNG 11 **Beantworte die folgenden Fragen schriftlich. Lies sie vorher gründlich durch und unterstreiche dann im Text die jeweiligen Textstellen. Beantworte die Fragen in vollständigen Sätzen in deinem Übungsheft.**

1. What is the weather like?
2. Where does Sarah want to go? Why?
3. Why is Sarah excited?
4. Where will she meet her mother?
5. What do we learn about Sarah's mother?
6. Why does Sarah like her father?
7. What does Yorkshire look like? (Take your atlas or a map of the British Isles and try to find Yorkshire!)

ÜBUNG 12 **Beantworte die folgenden Fragen, die über das Textverständnis hinausgehen. Bearbeite auch diese Fragen in vollständigen Sätzen in deinem Übungsheft.**

1. How would you describe Sarah?
2. Why do think Sarah hasn't visited her mother so far?
3. Do you think Sarah will come back to London?
4. Big city life or living in a village in the middle of nowhere – what do you like?

ÜBUNG 13 **Höre dir auf Track 10 der CD den Text über die Geschichte des Tower of London zweimal an und beantworte die Fragen in vollständigen Sätzen in deinem Übungsheft.**

10

Who began building the Tower of London?
What is the White Tower?
What was kept there during the Middle Ages?
Why are six to seven ravens still kept today?
How many tourists come every year to visit the Tower of London?
Who looks after the Tower of London today?
Why are they called Beefeaters?

ÜBUNG 14 **Höre dir auf Track 11 der CD den folgenden Text über Katies Reise zweimal an. Bearbeite dann die folgenden Aufgaben, indem du entscheidest, welche Aussagen wahr, welche falsch sind.**

11

	right	wrong
Katie is on a train from London to Aberdeen.	☐	☐
Katie's grandparents will collect her at the station in Aberdeen.	☐	☐
She is travelling with her parents.	☐	☐
She overslept so she couldn't have a proper breakfast.	☐	☐
She is looking for seat 52.	☐	☐
There is an old man sitting next to her.	☐	☐
The man helps her with her luggage.	☐	☐
She starts to listen to some music by a group called 'Milk and Honey'.	☐	☐

ÜBUNG 15 **Korrigiere die falschen Aussagen aus Übung 14 und schreibe sie korrekt auf. Höre dir, falls nötig, Track 11 auf der CD nochmals an.**

12

ÜBUNG 16 **Höre dir auf Track 12 der CD das Interview an, in dem Jack von Emma interviewt wird und beantworte anschließend die Fragen. Schreibe die richtigen Antworten in dein Übungsheft.**

Why is Emma interviewing Jack?
Where has Jack just been?
Why was he there?
How did he contact UNEP?
Why did he want to get involved in environmental issues?
What did he do at the Youth Forum?
What did Jack decide to do after he was in Blackpool?

13

ÜBUNG 17 **Höre dir auf Track 13 der CD die fünf Kurztexte zu einigen berühmten englischen Häfen zweimal an. Kreuze dann an, ob die folgenden Aussagen wahr oder falsch sind, und korrigiere die falschen Aussagen in deinem Übungsheft.**

	right	wrong
Plymouth can be found in Devon.	☐	☐
It is known as an historical place because it was invaded by Drake, Raleigh and Cook.	☐	☐
Mayflower is the name of a very famous ship.	☐	☐
Tenby is an attractive sea resort on the North Coast of Wales.	☐	☐
You can go shopping there in lovely shops, walking through narrow streets.	☐	☐
Liverpool is the biggest sea port in Great Britain.	☐	☐
Some dock buildings have been preserved.	☐	☐
Gloucester is famous because of its dome.	☐	☐
The canal in Gloucester, which was opened in 1872, made the city an important inland port.	☐	☐
There is a historic dock complex that can be visited.	☐	☐
Cornwall offers a mild climate for sub-tropical flowers.	☐	☐
Fishing is still a major source of income in Mevagissey.	☐	☐
When it becomes too busy there, the police close the village to motobikes.	☐	☐

9.3 Wörterbucharbeit

Das Wörterbuch als Arbeitsmittel

Für die Arbeit mit englischen Texten solltest du dir ein mittelgroßes **zweisprachiges Wörterbuch** anschaffen, um dich mit der Wörterbucharbeit vertraut zu machen.

Ein zweisprachiges Wörterbuch enthält folgende Informationen:

- die **Bedeutungen** eines Wortes,
- die Aussprache eines Wortes in **phonetischer Lautschrift** (einige Wörterbücher haben auch CD-ROMs mit der Aussprache),
- die **Silbentrennung,**
- die verschiedenen **Wortklassen** (z. B. Substantiv, Adjektiv, Verb), die meist durch Abkürzungen angezeigt werden.

homesick = Heimweh; salmon = Lachs
knee [niː], new [njuː], my [maɪ], island ['aɪlənd], lose [luːs]

fam-ily; home-work; bor-ing
dirty (adj. → Adjektiv), to choose (v. → Verb), book (n. → noun), trousers (pl. → Pluralwort)

Aufgepasst: Das Stichwort *(headword)* in einem Eintrag *(entry)* wird durch ein Auslassungszeichen, die **Tilde** (~), ersetzt.

hear: let me ~ from you – lassen Sie von sich hören
life: daily ~ – Alltagsleben

Zusatzinformationen im Wörterbuch

Weitere Inhalte sind

- **grammatikalische Besonderheiten** (z. B. die unregelmäßigen Formen eines Verbs),
- **Wendungen,**
- **Beispielsätze,**
- **Wortzusammensetzungen,**
- **Infokästen** zu Besonderheiten des Sprachgebrauchs oder bestimmten Themen oder hilfreiche **Bildtafeln.**

go, went *(past tense),* gone *(past participle)*

go into town – in die Stadt gehen,
to be out of town – nicht in der Stadt sein
place: He was placed second. – Er wurde Zweiter.
family: family name – Familienname,
car: car crash – Autounfall
useful phrases zu Themen wie “Saying thank you”, “Letter-writing”

ÜBUNG 18 **Schlage die folgenden Wörter nach und schreibe sie in der richtigen alphabetischen Reihenfolge in deinem Übungsheft auf.**

1. feet – fast – fashion – fan – favour – fault – fear – father
2. road – rise – ring – rink – right – ride
3. duck – dusty – dry – dummy – dying – drug
4. title – short – to – tip – near – neck – neighbour – war – underground

ÜBUNG 19 **Kreuze nach Kontrolle im Wörterbuch an, ob die Antwort richtig oder falsch ist. Wenn die Antwort falsch ist, verbessere sie in deinem Übungsheft.**

	richtig	falsch
“Advice” ist zählbar.	☐	☐
“To carry on” heißt „weitermachen“.	☐	☐
“Clean” ist ein Adjektiv.	☐	☐
“To look up” heißt „ein Wort nachschlagen“.	☐	☐
“Depend” wird mit der Präposition “of” benutzt.	☐	☐
“Platform” ist ein anderes Wort für „Bushaltestelle“.	☐	☐
Man sagt “to make a party” und nicht “to have a party”.	☐	☐

WISSEN

Besonderheiten der englischen Aussprache In vielen Wörtern gibt es **stumme** Laute, die nicht gesprochen werden.	listen, often, half, walk, sandwiches, two, knuckle, answer, autumn, biscuit, hour, grandpa, climb, guest
Achte auf die richtige Aussprache von [æ] und [e].	[æ]: cat, fat, hat, sat, flat, dad [e]: vet, fed, red, bed, bread, head
Vorsicht bei [w] und [v]: [w] wird ausgesprochen wie in *one*, [v] entspricht dem stimmhaften *w* wie in *Wasser*.	[w]: week, wet, Wednesday, with, will [v]: vet, evening, video, very, seven
Stimmloses oder stimmhaftes ***th?*** Präge dir die richtige Aussprache ein!	*stimmlos:* nothing, month, thanks, thing, mouth, healthy; *stimmhaft:* their, this, those, them, together

ÜBUNG 20 **Schlage die Aussprache der folgenden Wörter nach und unterstreiche den Buchstaben, der nicht ausgesprochen wird.**

knife – receipt – comb – castle – climb – knee

isle – salmon – tomb – knight – nose – sword

ÜBUNG 21 **Benutze dein Wörterbuch, um die Fragen zu beantworten.**

Was bedeutet "environment"?

Wie spricht man "weak", "weigh", "wilderness", "wine" aus?

Welches Substantiv lässt sich von "to choose" ableiten?

Welche Präposition(en) benutzt man mit "to protect"?

Welche zusammengesetzten Substantive kannst du unter dem Stichwort "summer" finden?

Wie sagt man auf Deutsch "What's the matter?"

Kannst du den feststehenden Ausdruck ergänzen? "trial and ______"

ÜBUNG 22 **Schlage das englische Wort *bar* nach und finde jeweils die deutsche Bedeutung.**

They've put bars in front of our window. →

We went to a bar in the centre of town. →

Could you get me a bar of chocolate? →

You have to order drinks at the bar. →

ÜBUNG 23 **In jedem Satz ist entweder ein falsches Wort oder eine falsche Präposition. Finde die richtige Lösung mittels eines Wörterbuches und verbessere den fehlerhaften Satz. Schreibe die Sätze in dein Übungsheft.**

ACHTUNG FEHLER

My mum was really worried with me.
Sarah isn't at home. She is by the doctor's.
This exercise is heavy.
That is typical for you.
We haven't been to the journey agent's yet to book our holidays.
The new shop is just round the edge.
This area is popular by tourists.

Klassenarbeit 1

60 Minuten

AUFGABE 1 **Lies die folgenden drei Texte aufmerksam durch.**

"Yesterday Died"
This is the 3rd James Colt movie and Fierce Mosman is starring in the role of the smart British agent 000. The evil guy this time is a media boss, who tries to start World War III.

Colt is called in to stop him and he is helped by a highly attractive elderly lady – Miss Garble, who can still use her sword (that's why friends and foes call her "The Swordfish"). Garble is madly in love with James (also dubbed "Jamie the Heartbreaker") and although having retired, she has always been eager to support 000.

Colt movie fans can expect all the same action and explosions in "Yesterday Died", but some things will be different, like Colt's car. In the other Colt movies the hero has driven a British-made sports car. This time Colt will be seen cycling – it's healthier and environmentally friendly.

"Mrs Pea"
Mrs Pea (Sarah Soft) is normally a quiet woman. She works at the National Gallery, a famous museum in London. All she has to do is to dust the expensive paintings. She has to make sure that the pictures are spotlessly clean, but most of the time she is in the broom closet, polishing her nails. She is not very good at her job and the others think that she is the laziest person who has ever worked for a museum.

Her bosses want to get rid of her. They decide to send her away on a mission to Hollywood to meet some very important people in America. And from this moment on Mrs Pea brings chaos (and flashy colours of nail polish) to the world.

TESTEN

"Gigantic"
The true story of the ship of dreams ... the Gigantic. The unsinkable tub. The great disaster. The secret in the north Atlantic Ocean. What stories of love and tragedy wait here to be told?

A beautiful woman. A poor, good-looking man. An expensive Polex watch. A true love that nothing on earth could stop. A collision with an iceberg that no-one could imagine.

See Leo diCapulet as Matt and Sadie Leaflet as Violet in the world's biggest dramatic romance. Don't miss it – it's a real tear jerker!

AUFGABE 2 **Wortschatzarbeit – finde das Gegenteil der folgenden Wörter.**

smart ↔

quiet ↔

poor ↔

elderly ↔

unsinkable ↔

expensive ↔

beautiful / good-looking ↔

AUFGABE 3 **Schlage folgende Wörter und Ausdrücke im Wörterbuch nach und übersetze sie ins Deutsche.**

to star a second time

a media boss

to be called in

to expect s.th.

to retire

tear jerker

to be good at

to get rid of s.b.

to imagine s.th.

broom closet

nail polish

AUFGABE 4 **Schreibe alle Wörter aus den drei Texten heraus, die du verstehen kannst, weil es im Deutschen ähnliche Ausdrücke gibt.**

"Yesterday Died":

"Mrs Pea":

"Gigantic":

AUFGABE 5 **Mache dir Notizen zu den drei Filmen: zur Geschichte, zu den Schauspielern, zu den Figuren. Lies dazu die Texte noch einmal und markiere die betreffenden Passagen.**

"Yesterday Died":

"Mrs Pea":

"Gigantic":

AUFGABE 6 **Würdest du einen dieser Filme sehen wollen? Warum? Warum nicht? Formuliere vier Sätze in deinem Übungsheft.**

Das 3-fach-Prinzip für bessere Noten:

Wissen • Üben • Testen

„Einfach klasse in“ – die Lernhilfe mit den drei Lernbausteinen und echten Klassenarbeiten für eine gezielte Vorbereitung!

Deutsch

Deutsch 5. Klasse
ISBN 978-3-411-72152-8

Deutsch 6. Klasse
ISBN 978-3-411-72162-7

Deutsch 7. Klasse
ISBN 978-3-411-72252-5

Deutsch 8. Klasse
ISBN 978-3-411-72262-4

Deutsch 9. Klasse
ISBN 978-3-411-72412-3

Deutsch 10. Klasse
ISBN 978-3-411-72422-2

Englisch

Englisch 5. Klasse
ISBN 978-3-411-72132-0

Englisch 6. Klasse
ISBN 978-3-411-72142-9

Englisch 7. Klasse
ISBN 978-3-411-72272-3

Englisch 8. Klasse
ISBN 978-3-411-72282-2

Englisch 9. Klasse
ISBN 978-3-411-72592-2

Englisch 10. Klasse
ISBN 978-3-411-72602-8

Mathematik

Mathematik 5. Klasse
ISBN 978-3-411-72172-6

Mathematik 6. Klasse
ISBN 978-3-411-72182-5

Mathematik 7. Klasse
ISBN 978-3-411-72432-1

Mathematik 8. Klasse
ISBN 978-3-411-72442-0

Mathematik 9. Klasse
ISBN 978-3-411-72572-4

Mathematik 10. Klasse
ISBN 978-3-411-72582-3

Französisch

Französisch 1. Lernjahr
ISBN 978-3-411-72742-1

Französisch 2. Lernjahr
ISBN 978-3-411-72752-0

Französisch 3./4. Lernjahr
ISBN 978-3-411-72822-0

Spanisch

Spanisch 1. Lernjahr
ISBN 978-3-411-73821-2

Spanisch 2. Lernjahr
ISBN 978-3-411-73811-3

Latein

Latein 1. Lernjahr
ISBN 978-3-411-72722-3

Latein 2. Lernjahr
ISBN 978-3-411-72732-2

Latein 3./4. Lernjahr
ISBN 978-3-411-72812-1

Jeder Band:

- 128 Seiten (Spanisch 96 Seiten)
- kartoniert
- mit Umschlagklappen

Stichwortfinder

STICHWORTFINDER